The Arno Press Cinema Program

A HISTORICAL STUDY OF THE ACADEMY OF MOTION PICTURE ARTS AND SCIENCES (1927-1947)

By

Pierre Norman Sands

ARNO PRESS

A NEW YORK TIMES COMPANY

New York • 1973

This volume was selected for the
Dissertations on Film Series
of the ARNO PRESS CINEMA PROGRAM
by Garth S. Jowett, Carleton University

First publication in book form, Arno Press, 1973

THE ARNO PRESS CINEMA PROGRAM
For complete listing of cinema titles see last pages

Manufactured in the United States of America

- -

Library of Congress Cataloging in Publication Data

Sands, Pierre Norman.
  A historical study of the Academy of Motion Picture
Arts and Sciences (1927-1947).

  (The Arno Press cinema program. Dissertations on
film series)
  Originally presented as the author's thesis,
University of Southern California, 1966.
    1. Academy of Motion Picture Arts and Sciences.
2. Academy awards (Moving-pictures) I. Title.
II. Series: The Arno Press cinema program. III.
Series: Dissertations on film series.
PN1993.A5S18 1972   791.43'06'273   72-557
ISBN 0-405-04100-4

A HISTORICAL STUDY OF THE ACADEMY OF

MOTION PICTURE ARTS AND SCIENCES

(1927-1947)

by

Pierre Norman Sands

―――――――

A Dissertation Presented to the

FACULTY OF THE GRADUATE SCHOOL

UNIVERSITY OF SOUTHERN CALIFORNIA

In Partial Fulfillment of the

Requirements for the Degree

DOCTOR OF PHILOSOPHY

(Cinema)

September 1966

TABLE OF CONTENTS

CHAPTER I

THE PROBLEM

Introduction

It is generally agreed that efforts at improvement
of the mass media must come from within the media
themselves or be generated by groups representing the
general public. Government can only play a minor role
in efforts to improve the media, if they are to
remain free. In each of the media there are organized
groups and individuals working for better performance:
trade associations, organizations of editors and
newsmen, professional societies, and outstanding individuals who have demonstrated leadership in responding
to the challenges raised by society.[1]

It is now generally accepted that motion pictures

have achieved the status of an art form unique in creation

and accomplished format from an inartistic beginning. In

---

[1]Edwin Emery, Phillip H. Ault, and Warren K. Agee,
Introduction to Mass Communications (New York: Dodd, Mead
Company, 1960), p. 157.

1

1915 Vachel Lindsay stated that motion pictures were sculpture, paintings, and architecture in motion.[2] In 1936 Allardyce Nicoll declared that motion pictures revealed depths of artistic expression even though they were designed to be popular. He contrasted motion pictures as permanent creations, like painting and sculpture, with the theatre where no two performances were given exactly alike. Nicoll further believed that theatre and motion pictures were basically similar in the element of movement, but emphasized that each individual frame of a film was a permanent record of compositional strength, beauty, and significance.[3] At about the same time Rudolph Arnheim had been developing his thesis of film as an art, which like painting, music, dance, and literature may or may not achieve artistic results with every production.[4] In 1950 Roger Manvell put forth his belief that the possibilities of motion pictures as a twentieth-century art form had been demonstrated by men like Griffith, Chaplin, Pudovkin, Lang, Eisenstein, Lubitsch,

---

[2]Vachel Lindsay, The Art of the Moving Picture (New York: The Macmillan Company, 1915), p. 4.

[3]Allardyce Nicoll, Film and Theatre (New York: Thomas Y. Crowell Company, 1936), pp. 38-41.

[4]Rudolph Arnheim, Film as Art (Berkeley and Los Angeles: University of California Press, 1957), p. 8.

Ford, and Rossellini.[5]

In 1927, the year that the Academy of Motion Picture Arts and Sciences was founded, all of the present mass media except television had significantly matured to influence public behavior. Motion pictures were established as a powerful mass medium even though they still lacked sound This imminent addition of sound to the already powerful visual medium was initially to set back artistic elements achieved thus far, but, when mastered, would bring films forward to even greater artistic heights in the years to come. This control of sound by the creative artist of motion pictures was indicated by William C. de Mille in 1931 when he stated:

> No longer is the microphone an impossibly severe and immovable master. Already we have reached the point where the use of the spoken word is producing a freer rather than a more restricted art form.[6]

Thus the actual development of the Academy of Motion Picture Arts and Sciences was to take place during a most significant portion of that time during which "the novelty

---

[5]Roger Manvell, Film (Rev. ed.; London: Hazell Watson and Viney, Ltd., 1950), p. 16.

[6]Lester Cowan (ed.), Recording Sound for Motion Pictures (New York: McGraw-Hill Book Company, Inc., 1931), p. v.

of 1895 has slowly been transformed into the art of the twentieth century."[7]

By 1927 there were indications that public interest in the silent film which had to rely on the moving visual for its communicative force was declining. The motion picture industry, as the fourth largest industry in America[8] with a product seen by millions of people all over the world, was under constant criticism for the alleged harmful influence of its product and for the examples of questionable personal conduct so eagerly publicized by the sensational press. In addition the industry was faced with both the need for further development and standardization of production equipment and techniques, and for achieving harmonious internal working relationships. The founders[9] of the Academy of Motion Picture Arts and Sciences responded to these societarian challenges by recognizing the desirability of forming a professional society composed of outstanding representatives from all facets of motion picture production

---

[7]Arthur Knight, The Liveliest Art (New York: The Macmillan Company, 1957), p. 11.

[8]Joseph P. Kennedy (ed.), The Story of the Films (New York: A. W. Shaw Company, 1927), p. 5.

[9]The thirty-six founders are listed in Appendix I.

who could work together to stimulate action in solution of these problems.

Public knowledge of the founders' efforts came about with the formal charter of the Academy on May 4, 1927 under the laws of the State of California, and at the organization banquet held on May 11, 1927.

Welford Beaton, President and Editor of the trade periodical The Film Spectator, was present at that banquet to hear the founders present the idea of the Academy to invited guests from industry, and commented in his paper:

> I felt as the evening grew that here were men and women worthy to bear the tremendous load of responsibility that the world had thrust upon them. They welded their power that night into an organization with possibilities more potential than even its sponsors can realize.[10]

The Problem

Statement of the Problem

The purpose of this study is to make a historical investigation of the Academy of Motion Picture Arts and Sciences and its contributions to education and the motion picture industry from 1927 to 1947.

---

[10] Welford Beaton, "Industry Fashioning Weapon of Defense," The Film Spectator, III, No. 7 (May 28, 1927), 3.

Importance of the Problem

A historical study of the Academy of Motion Picture Arts and Sciences is thought to be significant because: (1) the Academy is a unique non-profit honorary organization in the field of motion pictures; (2) it has attained international prestige over the years since its beginning in 1927; (3) it has made significant contributions to both education and the motion picture industry; (4) no such study of the Academy exists; and, (5) preliminary investigation has suggested that such a study might prove to be of additional value as the record of the type of organization coming from within a medium which aims at self-improvement.

In conducting a historical study of the Academy answers to specific questions were sought:

1. Why did the founders conceive of the need for a professional society composed of members of the motion picture industry?

2. Who were the founders, and were they truly representative of the entire motion picture industry?

3. What were the purposes, aims, and goals of the Academy, and how did they develop over the years?

4. What were the contributions of the Academy to education and to the motion picture industry?

5. What factors have led to the continued existence of the Academy as a non-profit organization which is not an official spokesman for the industry?

Limitations of the problem[11]

The beginning period of the Academy of Motion Picture Arts and Sciences has been emphasized to provide the proper perspective and understanding for its historical development and contributions. The study is concluded with the year 1947 since objective analysis of the period after that date is not yet possible.

Specific limitations were inherent in the material for this study in that the records of the development and operations of this private organization were largely confined to its own private files. Public interest has mostly been directed to that aspect of Academy functions devoted to

_____

[11] The emotional commitment of those individuals significantly involved with the Academy of Motion Picture Arts and Sciences and their common experience, unique to the profession, of having any published statement avidly seized on and warped out of context, made personal interviews almost entirely unproductive.

the presentation of achievement awards to members of the
motion picture industry.

Review of Literature

There has been considerable mention made of the
Academy of Motion Picture Arts and Sciences in the printed
media; however, these have been almost entirely concerned
with the awards for achievement. Practically no factual
and historical material on the Academy exists outside of
that maintained within its own private files. Verification
of printed Academy material, such as bulletins, has been
done from unpublished records in the Academy's own files
where necessary. The Bibliography for this study lists all
pertinent references believed necessary to provide the proper prespective for understanding the Academy development and
contributions in relation to the motion picture industry and
the period during which the Academy was founded.

One Doctoral dissertation, published as Stars and
Strikes by Murray Ross of Columbia University, contains
information related to this study. Ross was concerned with
the development of the motion picture industry unions, and
mentions the actions of the Academy of Motion Picture Arts
and Sciences in its efforts to promote harmonious industrial

relationships within the industry.[12]

There seems to have been no other studies which relate to this dissertation. This is based on: a review of all studies reported in the Audio Visual Communications Review and Speech Monographs; all theses and dissertations listed in Dissertation Abstracts; and the absence of any reference to such studies in the literature.

Procedure

A review of all available literature, including an examination of official records in the private files of the Academy of Motion Picture Arts and Sciences, was made; discussions were held with numerous persons associated with the Academy. The International Index to Periodicals, Library Literature Index, Reader's Guide to Periodical Literature, and the Educational Index were checked. Recognizing that minor references to the Academy of Motion Picture Arts and Sciences, particularly in the founding days, might not appear in such indices a careful search was made of such publications as The Saturday Review of Literature, The Film Spectator, Motion Picture Herald, Rob Wagner's

---

[12]Murray Ross, Stars and Strikes (New York: Columbia University Press, 1941).

Script, Moving Picture World, The International Motion Picture Almanac, The Film Index, The Film Daily Year Book of Motion Pictures, Variety, Daily Variety, Transactions of the Society of Motion Picture Engineers, Theatre Arts Monthly, the New York Times and the Los Angeles Times. All information accumulated from these sources was carefully evaluated in terms of this study.

A serious problem was presented in deciding upon the best manner for presentation of the accumulated data so that it would clearly and most meaningfully achieve the purpose of the dissertation. For example, a straightforward chronological record of the Academy beginnings, development, and contributions would serve only to confuse the relationships among past events. Therefore the separation of data into three sections devoted to highlights of the Academy development, contributions to the motion picture industry, and contributions to education came as the logical solution. Further, no historical study is valid if conducted in disregard of cultural context; therefore achievement of a true perspective required a separate section devoted to the times which acted as a stimulus on the Academy founders. The history of motion pictures, including the technical state of the art, the impact of unions on the motion picture industry, and concerns for the threat of censorship have all been repeatedly covered in the literature. However, within this section it was necessary to provide some emphasis to those facets of this material which appeared to have influenced the Academy founders.

Organization of the Remainder of the Dissertation

Chapter II establishes the climate of the times in America under which the Academy founders reacted to form their professional society. The historical development of the Academy, in terms of key organizational elements, is provided in Chapter III. Contributions made by the Academy to education are covered in Chapter IV, and those to the motion picture industry in Chapter V. The summary and conclusions drawn from the foregoing chapters are contained in Chapter VI. The Bibliography provides a listing of material cited, and also includes references to education, motion pictures, and the communications media in general which were pertinent to the investigations conducted during this study. The Appendix provides additional details considered of value to this study.

CHAPTER II

HISTORICAL PERSPECTIVE OF THE FOUNDING PERIOD

OF THE ACADEMY OF MOTION PICTURE

ARTS AND SCIENCES

The thirty-six founders of the Academy were all
born in the 1880's and 1890's, and rose to eminence in the
motion picture industry during a period of American history
that was particularly dynamic. The impact of conditions in
America, including that of all the relatively young mass
media of communications, upon them as individuals in turn
influenced their decisions in creating what has become a
world-recognized and esteemed organization related to this
twentieth-century art form. The founders were not merely
a product of the times, but instead they helped mold the
times through the communications medium known as the motion
picture. People were their commodity, and what these
people thought and did was of prime interest and particular
importance to them. To understand the motivations and

actions of these men and women in founding the Academy and, through it, influencing and participating in the critical transition from silent to sound films and the maturing of the industry, it is necessary to appreciate the contemporary social milieu and public attitudes.

The United States of America was the strongest economic and military power in the world at the end of World War I. A minor economic slump occurred after the War followed by a short business boom which lasted until the middle of 1920. The depression of 1921 ended with business recovery in 1922 and a state of prosperity that lasted until 1929. This prosperity was largely built on new and expanding industries for construction and the production of such items as the automobile, chemicals, household appliances, and radios. The number of wage earners in the United States doubled during the 1920's.[1] Competition for economic profit was keen, and the Americans made notable additions during these years to all fields of scientific knowledge. There were increased numbers of women in occupations that had been traditionally masculine; established social patterns

---

[1]Gilbert C. Fite and Jim E. Reese, An Economic History of the United States (Boston: Houghton Mifflin Company, 1952), pp. 524-532.

were in a state of flux. The national attitudes of the time
can be summarized as a state of continuous euphoria, bound-
less self-confidence, and instinctive revolt against traditional forms and ethics. Individuals were primarily concerned with their own goals and desires; they evinced such
lack of empathy as to amount almost to callousness toward
the problems of others.

By 1927, radio, as a competing medium, had achieved
vast influence and a degree of maturity. Listeners no longer searched among the frequencies for entertainment, but
developed loyalties to personalities. Obscure announcers
and singers became public idols. Radio had moved rapidly
ahead since the days of 1920 when it was thought of primarily as a message service handicapped by its lack of privacy.
A year later, in 1921, the public had bought or built millions of sets, and in response, new stations were springing
up in hotels and stores. Broadcasting was completely uncon-
trolled and very informal. By 1922 the monetary implica-
tions were obvious; the American Society of Composers,
Authors and Publishers demanded royalties, and a New York
station inaugurated the new practice of selling radio time
for advertising. Despite the protests of magazines and
newspapers the practice spread quickly, until the size of

the industry and social pressures required establishment of

the Federal Radio Commission (superseded in 1934 by the

Federal Communications Commission) to regulate the airwaves

in the public interest.[2]

By 1927 newspapers, magazines, and books all were

prosperous businesses, each with a mass audience. News-

papers had their press associations, newspaper chains, syn-

dicated news, comic strips (which made semi-reading easy

for the immigrant, farmer, and worker), and the use of the

half-tone process to reproduce photos. The early fears

that motion pictures would eliminate reading proved to be

ill-founded, and newspapers, at first hostile to movies,

began to feature film news to increase their own circula-

tion. A new industry for "fan" magazines had appeared;

when Hollywood reproduced a classic on film the public

libraries had excessive demands for the book versions.[3]

Isolation of families and communities within the

United States had been broken down by automobiles, news-

papers, and radio. However, there was a return to the

[2]Erik Barnouw, Mass Communication: Television, Radio, Film, Press (New York: Rinehart and Company, Inc., 1956), pp. 29-33.

[3]Ibid., p. 24.

strong isolationism--in an international sense--of earlier
years and a resurgent nationalism which vented itself in
carrying out attacks on history and social-science text-
books in the schools. Nevertheless, better schools afforded greater opportunities to rural children, and undeniable
contributions were made in raising the cultural level of
the nation. The most important gain was in education where
the outstanding achievement was to make secondary education
almost as universal as primary education had become in the
past century. To make this possible, the cost of education
doubled between 1920 and 1926. The old fashioned one-room
school was no longer sufficient. Instead schools were ac-
quiring laboratories, gymnasiums, libraries, auditoriums,
playgrounds, and lunchrooms. With the development of 16mm
film, and the production of educational films for classroom
use, visual education began to play a more important role
in the 1920's. College enrollment rose from 26,654 in 1910
to 462,445 in 1920, to 868,793 in 1928, and to over a million in 1935. By the middle twenties the average American
believed young people had as much right to a college education as high school training.[4] After World War I most of

[4]Harold Underwood Faulkner, American Political and
Social History (New York: Appleton-Century-Crofts, Inc.,
1952), pp. 711-726.

the liberal arts colleges had a curriculum pattern which
followed the accepted bodies of organized knowledge. Thus
there was a traditional subject matter curriculum organized
by departments such as history, economics, physics, chemis-
try, English, botany, astronomy, and foreign languages.[5]
However, since our universities and colleges, unlike the
European, lack the monastic traditions and were established
to serve, rather than stand aloof from social needs, curric-
ula have been modified to provide specific training as well
as traditional education.

A tremendous immigration wave of over a million individuals each year in 1905, 1906, and 1907 had arrived to
live in American city slums. Since most could not read
English, they formed an eager mass market for the nickelodeons, cultivating a taste which supported later developments.[6] In 1908 D. W. Griffith startled his audiences with
new techniques, and the art of motion pictures was begun.
By 1914 films were in world-wide demand. European studios
were affected by the war, and the American film industry

[5]R. Freeman Butts and Lawrence A Cremin, A History of Education in American Culture (New York: Henry
Holt and Company, 1953), pp. 595-596.

[6]Barnouw, op. cit., pp. 17-19.

began to supply the world's theatres. Hollywood became the world's film capital by 1917.

Although the national cultural level was yet largely determined by the schools and the press, the motion picture and the radio had begun to share in the moulding of American civilization. By the end of the 1920's, 23,000 motion picture theatres with an aggregate seating capacity of 11,000,000 were playing to some 100,000,000 people a week. The Hollywood motion picture industry was turning out about 500 feature films and hundreds of shorts each year.[7]

This world leadership in motion picture production was not without its drawbacks. Even in the early days, the nickelodeons' obsession with the sensational had brought about denunciations from public elements and now, with such a volume of product reaching even larger audiences, all sorts of interests--governmental, political, financial, and religious--began to concern themselves with Hollywood's productions. All were anxious to show the film producers how to use, or how not to use, their apparent power over the people. Criticisms of the film industry, its product,

---

[7]Faulkner, op. cit., p. 728.

and people, constituted no small part of the public attention to Hollywood. Although some criticism was admittedly justified, there was a strong feeling among many in the industry that it was exaggerated.

The producers became more and more sensitive to controversy, and were afraid of alienating any large segment of their huge market. In fear of official censorship the film producers engaged Will H. Hays in 1922 to head a program of self-control within the industry. Hays had been the Postmaster General under President Harding, and the producers believed that under his name, their program would calm the rising tide of adverse criticism. The motion picture industry in Hollywood, under the direction of Hays, developed a system of self-censorship which was later strengthened by a formal production code. All this, however, did not succeed in eliminating outside interference. A few states and some cities had set up local censorship boards to pass on motion pictures, and these continued to reject films in spite of prior clearance by the Hays office. Religious and other groups maintained committees to review films and publish ratings of approval or disapproval.[8]

---

[8]Barnouw, op. cit., p. 20.

It is ironic to note that while the motion picture

industry sought to avoid adverse criticism and censorship,

factors within the industry would operate in such a manner

as to bring about undesirable attention. The studios often

resorted to extreme publicity techniques just to capture

public attention and hopefully achieve increased receipts

at the box-offices. In discussing the industry in the

1920's Arthur Knight stated:

> Whole departments were added to feed tidbits of
> information to the newspapers and to the increasing-
> ly important fan magazines. No stunt was too out-
> landish, no "angle" too improbable, if it might
> capture a front-page headline or a magazine feature
> story for the studio's current darlings.[9]

To make matters worse some of these individuals began to

believe their own publicity, and having gained wealth and

public acclaim thought they could do no wrong. They became

involved in sensational episodes which were avidly printed

by the press. These factors combined to give Hollywood and

the motion picture industry a dual and somewhat conflicting

reputation for corruptness and glamor.[10]

As Hollywood became the major center for motion

---

[9]Arthur Knight, The Liveliest Art (New York: The
Macmillan Company, 1957), p. 108.

[10]Ibid., p. 111.

picture production after World War I it represented a prime target for unionization. "Hollywood was to become a Trojan horse by means of which organized labor would penetrate anti-union Los Angeles."[11] This was logical since many of the studio crafts, such as the electricians and carpenters, were to be found in the local industries. The American Federation of Labor made its first attempt with some success in 1916 to unionize the studio crafts. This drive by union forces "awakened motion picture producers to the existence of a labor problem which required handling by a single agency representing all producers."[12] The formation of the Motion Picture Producers' Association "marked the beginning of a unified labor policy among Hollywood's major film producers."[13]

In the spring of 1918 the Alliance of Theatrical Stage Employes and Motion Picture Machine Operators, an affiliate of the American Federation of Labor, began a drive to unionize all stage crafts. Jurisdictional disputes over the studio crafts arose between the Alliance and the major craft unions of the American Federation of Labor.

---

[11]Murray Ross, Stars and Strikes (New York: Columbia University Press, 1941), pp. 5-6.

[12]Ibid., p. 6.   [13]Ibid., p. 7.

These disputes were not to be settled until 1926. In the meantime the motion picture industry had undergone two strikes by studio craftsmen and one minor strike by camera-men between 1918 and 1921. With the settlement of the union jurisdictional disputes, the producers faced the pos-sibility of a unified general strike. This caused them to sign the first union agreement, known as the Studio Basic Agreement,[14] which covered the stagehands, carpenters, painters, electricians, and musicians.[15]

Actors' Equity Association was given union juris-diction over all screen players in 1920 by the Associated Actors and Artists of America. Equity then actively sought to gain recognition by the motion picture industry, and thus strengthen their position with the legitimate theatre. How-ever, at this time the screen actors, many of whom lacked stage experience, were not particularly interested in join-ing Equity. This was simply because the abuses facing stage actors were not common in the motion picture industry, and screen actors were relatively content with their current

[14]The Studio Basic Agreement has been renewed and continues to function without major disturbances.

[15]Ross, op. cit., pp. 7-14.

working relationships. Equity paused in its efforts to organize the screen actors, but kept an interest in the motion picture industry. In 1922 Equity unsuccessfully attempted to negotiate a standard contract with the motion picture producers. Equity's next move occurred in 1924 with the publication of alleged abuses by certain studios. Despite Equity's claim for credit when the studio practices were improved they failed to win the screen actors' support for an Equity standard contract with the producers.[16]

The Authors' League of America, which was organized in 1912, began to interest its members in writing for the motion picture industry. They offered the members assistance in matters of plagiarism, and in obtaining proper individual contracts. Affiliation of this group in 1916 with the American Federation of Labor to gain the support of organized labor was prevented by its own members. In the meantime the Photoplay Authors' League was established in Hollywood in 1914 as an independent group simply because the Authors' League of America was located in the East. The Photoplay Authors' League campaigned against fake scenario-writing schools, and worked to protect its members'

---

[16]Ibid., pp. 23-27.

copyrights. Although successful in these areas the Photoplay Authors' League proved ineffectual in attempting to
protect the professional standing of writers. In the early
days of the motion picture industry writers prepared short
scenarios which the directors changed to suit their purposes. By 1920 writers were preparing scripts for feature
length films, and many were established authors. These
individuals, not wanting to be treated like early scenario
writers, established the Screen Writers' Guild of the
Authors' League of America to represent them. Anyone writing for motion pictures was eligible for membership in the
Guild; however, membership was by invitation only. The
Guild, from 1920 through 1926, was to provide valuable services for its members, improve the writer-producer relationships, cooperate with the Hays office in campaigning
against censorship, but was unable to obtain a standard
contract with producers for the writers.[17]

In 1926, the year before the Academy of Motion Picture Arts and Sciences was founded, motion picture production had become fairly complex. It was no longer a simple
matter of three or four people getting together to make a

[17]Ibid., pp. 48-54.

film. Studio organization had already developed requirements for business executives in cost accounting, legal ad-
vice, and public relations, and scores of technical special-
ties were appearing. The forerunners of today's cinematographers, editors, costume designers, art directors, sound
engineers and many other craftsmen were in evidence although
they were generally considered under the title of "technicians."

P. M. Abbott, Vice-President of the Society of
Motion Picture Engineers, stated in 1946 that "few industries make such varied and difficult demands from the standpoint of mechanical equipment as does the motion picture
trade."[18] Studio equipment included cameras costing three
to five thousand dollars with a "great variety of footage
counters, punches, focusing devices and trick attachments
of every description and the greatest complexity."[19] Lighting equipment consisted of a combination of carbon arcs for
hard lighting, and the Cooper-Hewitt mercury vapor lamps
for soft lighting. The carbon arcs included spot lights,

---

[18] P. M. Abbott, "Equipment Used for Motion Pictures," The Annals of the American Academy of Political and
Social Science, CXXVIII (November, 1926), 34.

[19] Ibid., pp. 36-38.

baby spot lights, broadsides, overhead dome lights, and other mountings for special effects. Set construction used a variety of mechanical devices and special techniques from machine shops, carpenter shops, plaster shops, metal-working departments, and dressmaking workrooms. Studios had their own power plants, including portable units for location shooting.[20] Most of the technical developments were carefully guarded within the individual studios, although some exchange of knowledge occurred through commercial manufacturers and such organizations as the American Society of Cinematographers and the Society of Motion Picture Engineers. K. C. D. Hickman. Research Chemist at the Research Laboratory of Eastman Kodak Company, commented on this situation early in 1927:

> Since there is keen rivalry as between studio and studio, reserve must be practiced over technical working details. It is indeed a great tribute to the technicians that in spite of the immediate danger many are long-sighted enough to speak openly of their work, that bread cast upon the waters may return to them and their brethren after many days.[21]

Two important factors in consideration of the

---

[20]Ibid.

[21]K. C. D. Hickman, "Hollywood and the Motion Picture Engineers," Transactions of the Society of Motion Picture Engineers, XI (April, 1927), 34.

period just prior to the founding of the Academy of Motion
Picture Arts and Sciences are the indications of a declining
public interest in the silent film and the advent of sound.

Kenneth Macgowan wrote:

> To hold the audience, America's first-run exhibitors
> added symphony orchestras and vaudeville; and they
> fused these into what they called "presentations" or
> "prologs." For an hour, film audiences watched
> revues with singers, comics, vaudeville acts, elabo-
> rate scenery, and a teeming chorus of dancing girls
> whose mechanical perfection would put a millepede to
> shame. In spite of all this, the size of the audiences
> shrank.[22]

Since 1923 De Forest had been using sound-on-film,
called Phonofilm, with a series of shorts on vaudeville
personalities. However, "they caused little stir in the
industry."[23] On August 6, 1926 Warner Brothers and the
Vitaphone Corporation showed the silent feature film
Don Juan, which had a synchronized orchestral accompaniment
on disc. The feature was preceded by a series of shorts
with synchronized sound on disc which included Will Hays
giving a talk, songs by Marion Talley, Anna Case, and
Martinelli, and violin pieces by Mischa Elman and Zimbalist.
"As far as the motion picture industry is concerned, sound

---

[22]Kenneth Macgowan, Behind the Screen (New York:
Delacorte Press, 1965), p. 283.

[23]Knight, op. cit., p. 146.

came that night to the silent screen."[24] Sidney R. Kent,

General Manager of Famous Players-Lasky Corporation, wrote

an article that same year about the future of motion pic-

tures in which he noted the importance of this production

of Don Juan:

> Now playing on Broadway is a marvellous piece of
> mechanism known as Vitaphone. Through it the music
> of the symphony orchestras, the songs of noted opera
> stars, will be available to audiences in the smallest
> hamlet.[25]

Despite this achievement by Warners the "audiences

were interested--nothing more."[26] In January of 1927 Fox

demonstrated an improved sound-on-film, and in April of

that same year released the first Movietone newsreel which

was an immediate success. However not until six months

later, just after the founding date of the Academy of

Motion Picture Arts and Sciences, were both audiences and

producers convinced that sound was here to stay. On that

date Warners released The Jazz Singer, which contained a

---

[24]Lester Cowan (ed.), Recording Sound for Motion
Pictures (New York: McGraw-Hill Book Company, Inc., 1931),
p. 10.

[25]Sidney R. Kent, "The Motion Picture of Tomorrow,"
The Annals of the American Academy of Political and Social
Science, CXXVIII (November, 1926), 32-33.

[26]Knight, loc. cit.

few lines of dialogue and several songs by Al Jolson.
Jolson was what sound needed--"the spark, the flame that
would kindle the public's imagination and enthusiasm."[27]
"The success of the film told other producers that they must
turn to sound."[28]

The rapid growth of industrial America, the increased education of its people; the rapidity with which information and editorial opinions could be spread throughout
the country; the world leadership position of the Hollywood
motion picture industry; the need for sharing technical
developments and techniques; the dwindling public interest
in the silent films; the appearance of sound films on the
horizon; the problems of unionism; and the extent of public
criticism directed at the motion picture industry represented the period and the conditions which were reflected in the
ideas of the founders of the Academy of Motion Picture Arts
and Sciences when they thought to establish a professional
society which might work toward the betterment of the
motion picture industry.

---

[27] Ibid., p. 147.

[28] Macgowan, op. cit., p. 284.

CHAPTER III

HISTORICAL DEVELOPMENT OF THE ACADEMY OF
MOTION PICTURE ARTS AND SCIENCES

The organization of the Academy of Motion Picture
Arts and Sciences consisted of different groups, each with
equal representation on the Board of Governors (later
called Board of Directors), and each group with a semi-
autonomous branch organization of its own. This diverse
representation tended to provide a balanced opinion representing the considered judgment of all groups. These
groups were part of the Academy which was an exclusive, invitational, honorary organization, and their opinions and
actions were those of the organization, not of the entire
motion picture industry per se. The Academy reacted to
situations within the motion picture industry as they
occurred, and within the framework of the organization
took action for the betterment of the situations.[1]

---

[1]M. C. Levee, one of the founders and third President of the Academy of Motion Picture Arts and Sciences.
Taped interview, January, 1966.

The Academy underwent certain changes in organization and in functions performed during the period covered
by this study. A considerable number of the changes were
simply the natural result of organizational growth, but
others were due to external circumstances of the moment.
Early attention given to countering unwarranted public
criticism was dropped almost immediately, and never became
a major factor in Academy functions.[2] Awards of Merit
steadily gained in importance until by 1947 they were to be
a predominant Academy function. The technical activities
of the Academy carried through the entire period achieving
an impressive record of contributions to the motion picture
industry including the sponsorship of research, development
of new techniques and standards, and the sharing of technical knowledge. The Academy made many contributions to education both inside and outside the motion picture industry
in responding to situations as they arose. Efforts to
achieve harmonious working relationships, although successful in certain facets of the motion picture industry's
labor problems,[3] ended in 1937 when the Academy revised its

[2]Ibid.

[3]Murray Ross, Stars and Strikes (New York: Columbia University Press, 1941), p. 215.

By-Laws to withdraw from all labor-management matters. This
aspect of Academy activity, covered in Chapter V of this
study, pages 202-226, lasted for ten years and stimulated
controversy, leaving a record of allegations that it was
a "company union" founded and controlled by the producers.

Nevertheless, individuals most intimately connected
with the formation and operation of the Academy agree that
such statements are unfounded. Bosley Crowther's belief[4]
that Louis B. Mayer conceived of the idea to form the
Academy specifically to achieve goals of the producers, and
such statements as the one by Murray Ross that the "producers established the Academy of Motion Picture Arts and
Sciences,"[5] are vigorously denied by Conrad Nagel.[6] Another
reference by Ross that "there is little exaggeration in
Equity's claim that the producers controlled the destinies
of the Academy,"[7] is not borne out by the Academy records.
Ross based his statement on the fact that of two sub-

---

[4]Bosley Crowther, Hollywood Rajah (New York: Dell
Publishing Company, Inc., 1960), pp. 199-202.

[5]Ross, op. cit., p. 27.

[6]Conrad Nagel. Personal correspondence, January
21, 1966. Interview, January 30, 1966.

[7]Ross, op. cit., p. 41.

categories of active members in 1930 only the Foundation
members were eligible for election to the Board of Directors. He implies that the Foundation members were the producers, whereas in fact they had the same composition of
writers, directors, actors, and technicians as did the
Academy members. These two sub-categories of members
(Foundation and Academy) came into being in February 1930
simply to make it financially easier for some individuals
to belong to the Academy of Motion Picture Arts and Sciences. The fact that the intent of the Board of Directors
was not to create a class of members who would be unable to
participate in Academy management is clearly evident in
their repeated statements to the contrary.

Founding Period

During the first week of January 1927 Fred Niblo,
a prominent motion picture director, and Conrad Nagel, a
distinguished actor, were having dinner at the Santa Monica
home of L. B. Mayer, a notable producer. Niblo and Nagel
had been discussing the motion picture industry, and the
fact that "attacking Hollywood was the favorite indoor
sport of reform organizations and censorship groups at that

time."[8] They went on to agree that "there was no unified voice representing the entire industry to speak out against these attacks."[9] Motion pictures had gained stature both as a large industry and as a field of influential creative art, and yet there was no single organization composed of outstanding craftsmen representative of the entire industry In those days the editors, art directors, and cinematographers were all grouped under the general term of technicians. Thus Niblo and Nagel considered that representation of the entire motion picture industry could be accomplished by groups or categories of writers, actors, directors, producers, and technicians.[10]

Niblo, who had been a stage star as well as a director, and Nagel both had a long record of activity in organizing actors, particularly in connection with the Actors' Equity Association. It was therefore quite natural for them to think in terms of organizing a group of people from the motion picture industry to work in its behalf. Mayer thought they had a good idea, and said that if they could gather a representative group from industry he would arrange a dinner for them the following week at which

---

[8]Nagel, loc. cit.   [9]Ibid.   [10]Ibid.

time the idea could be discussed.   Such a discussion would

determine if there was any merit in having such an organi-

zation.[11]

The following day Niblo, Nagel, and Mayer contacted

various individuals whom they believed to be outstanding in

the motion picture industry.   They explained the basic idea,

and invited them to the dinner to be held at the Ambassador

Hotel on the evening of January 11, 1927.   A few of those

who were invited asked others in their category to attend.

Not all of the individuals who were invited[12] came to the

dinner, but those who did--including Niblo, Nagel, and

Mayer--totaled thirty-six.[13]   Niblo and Nagel had not been

concerned with numbers of individuals, but rather with

getting together a sufficient number of outstanding indi-

viduals who were representative of the industry and who

would be willing to work for establishment of the proposed

organization.[14]   In addition to representing a cross-

---

[11]Ibid.

[12]There is no record of those invited, nor can
Nagel or Levee recall exactly who they were.

[13]These became the founders of the Academy who are
listed in Appendix I.

[14]Nagel, loc. cit.

section of the categories of the motion picture industry as
defined by the nature of their work, these individuals
(founders) also varied widely in their background, education, and the manner in which they came into the industry.
Eleven of the thirty-six had college degrees, which was a
relatively high average for their age group in America.
Some had been educated abroad, others were the products of
special schools, and still others were typical of the self-
educated, self-made men of that era.

At the dinner on the evening of January 11, 1927
the founders were all enthusiastic about Niblo's and Nagel's
idea. Each spoke informally in terms of his or her particular interest and activity, explaining where they believed
such an organization might be of benefit to the motion picture industry. At the conclusion of the evening all had
agreed to gather in informal meetings to work out the details for establishing the organization. There were to be
many such informal meetings[15] resulting in the plans for
the Academy as expressed in the Constitution and By-Laws
adopted on May 5, 1927.

It was at this dinner, or one of the later informal

---

[15]Levee, loc. cit.

sessions, that Nagel suggested that the organization be
called the "Academy of Motion Picture Arts and Sciences
International." The founders discussed this suggestion at
some length, and finally decided to drop the word "International." To them the title "Academy of Motion Picture
Arts and Sciences" reflected their convictions that the
organization should represent all facets of motion picture
production both in the arts and the sciences. They also
believed that this particular title would properly reflect
the dignity and honor of a profession considered by them to
be the equal of other creative fields of endeavor.[16]

By the 19th of March the founders had selected
their first officers and Board of Directors,[17] whom they
agreed would hold office only until a general election
could be held, and had presented articles of incorporation[18]
to a Notary Public in Los Angeles County. On May 4, 1927
a charter for the Academy of Motion Picture Arts and Sciences was granted under California laws. With the collection of admission fees from the thirty-six founders suffi-

---

[16]Nagel, op. cit.

[17]Listed in Appendix II.

[18]Articles of Incorporation of Academy of Motion
Picture Arts and Sciences, dated March 19, 1927.

cient funds existed to defray the costs involved, including
holding an organization banquet. The banquet was scheduled
for May 11, 1927 by the founders who hoped to attract
enough interest to start the Academy with a basic membership of outstanding individuals representative of all five
categories in the motion picture industry.[19]

Organization Banquet

The founders held the organization banquet for the
Academy of Motion Picture Arts and Sciences on May 11, 1927
at the Biltmore Hotel in Los Angeles. To this banquet they
invited 300 men and women from the motion picture industry.
They selected for invitation those individuals whom they
believed met the criteria established in the Constitution
and By-Laws for membership.[20] Each invitation gave a
summary of the founders' reasons for forming the Academy
with the promise that their aims and objectives would be
more fully explained at the banquet. The banquet invitation set forth in part:

> If we producing workers, actors, directors, tech-
> nicians, cinematographers and producing executives,
> who have the future progress of this great universal
> entertainment at heart, will now join unselfishly

[19]Levee, loc. cit.   [20]Ibid.

into one big concerted movement, we will be able
to effectually accomplish those essential things
which we have hitherto neglected. We can take
aggressive action in meeting outside attacks that
are unjust. We can promote harmony and solidarity
among our membership and among our different branches.
We can reconcile any internal differences that may
exist or arise. We can adopt such ways and means as
are proper to further the welfare and protect the
honor and good repute of our profession. We can encourage the improvement and advancement of the arts
and sciences of our profession by the interchange of
constructive ideas and by awards of merit for distinctive achievements. We can take steps to develop
the greater power and influence of the screen.[21]

Thirteen of the founders spoke at this banquet.

Welford Beaton, publisher and editor of The Film Spectator,

quoted Cecil B. de Mille as emphasizing that the group

attending this banquet "constituted the most powerful group

ever assembled in the world, a group that influences the

mental processes of all mankind."[22] In the same article

Beaton gave the highest praise to a speech by Conrad Nagel:

I have heard great orators in several parts of the
world, but in all my experience I have heard none
deliver an address more notable for its logic, for
its choice of words, for its diction, enunciation
and good taste, than that delivered by Conrad Nagel,
a motion picture actor.[23]

---

[21] Invitation to the Organization Banquet of the
Academy of Motion Picture Arts and Sciences, May 11, 1927.

[22] Welford Beaton, "Industry Fashioning Weapon of
Defense," The Film Spectator, III, No. 7 (May 28, 1927), 3.

[23] Ibid.

In a second article Beaton expressed his overall
reaction:

> Every branch of production is represented on its
> board of directors and the best brains in the indus-
> try are at the service of the most unimportant person
> connected with it. It is an organization founded in
> a spirit of trust and confidence, and as long as it
> is credited with living up to its ideals it will be
> of vast benefit to those whom it unselfishly seeks
> to serve. No one group, or two groups in collusion,
> can control it. That it will not be successful is
> unthinkable.[24]

An article in The Film Daily commented:

> Enthusiasm marked the invitation banquet last night
> at which the Academy of Motion Picture Arts and
> Sciences was formed. The new organization, of which
> Douglas Fairbanks is the president, it was predicted,
> will revolutionize relations between various factors
> of the industry, particularly in promotion.[25]

The enthusiasm of the invited guests was reflected
in the large number (231) who became members of the Academy
that evening. It had been made clear to all of them that
they were there as dinner guests of the founders and were
under no obligation, but that if they would like to participate in the organization they could join. The admission
fees collected that evening by the Treasurer,

---

[24]Welford Beaton, "Is Entitled to Support of All,"
The Film Spectator, III, No. 7 (May 28, 1927), 4.

[25]Film Daily, XL, No. 36 (May 12, 1927), 3.

M. C. Levee,[26] enabled the Academy to begin operations on a solid financial ground. They could rent office space, employ stenographers, and meet initial expenses.[27]

Constitution and By-Laws

The ultimate success of any committee or organization rests to a large degree on the manner in which the Constitution and By-Laws are prepared. In particular a Constitution must provide for the purpose of the organization, and the method for election of officials. The basis for future arguments, because of ambiguities, must be minimized.

In this respect the Academy was fortunate in having the original Constitution and By-Laws drafted in a form which assured proper functioning of the organization and yet permitted necessary amendments to keep pace with its growth, changes in functions performed, and development without weakening the basic structure.

----

[26]M. C. Levee had been selected by the other founders to be the Treasurer because of his experience in raising funds for the motion picture industry. He had been Treasurer of the Motion Picture Relief Fund, Treasurer of the exclusive Mayfair Club, and the first Chairman of the Community Chest Drive in the motion picture industry.

[27]Levee, loc. cit.

Early recognition of this fact was given in one of the first Academy information bulletins which indicated that "the success of the Academy's operations are largely due to the sound foundation of the well worked-out Constitution."[28] The bulletin went on to pay tribute from all members to Edwin Loeb and George Cohen "for their untiring and able services, voluntarily tendered, in drafting the Constitution and By-Laws."[29] Using a standard pattern Loeb and Cohen worked with the founders embodying agreed upon ideas, concepts, and methods for what they all "hoped the Academy would become."[30]

The original form of the Constitution provided for such matters as: purposes of the organization; membership, including fees and dues; order of business, and the use of parliamentary procedure at meetings; duties and responsibilities of the officials and committees; provisions for amendments; and methods for election of Academy officials.

Between the time of the adoption of the Constitution and By-Laws on May 5, 1927 and 1947, a period of

---

[28] Academy of Motion Picture Arts and Sciences, Bulletin, No. 2, June 17, 1927, p. 2.

[29] Ibid.

[30] Nagel, loc. cit.

twenty years, it was to be changed and amended only twelve
times.

By February 10, 1930 five amendments had been made
which were of a relatively minor nature pertaining to fees
and dues, and the division of Active members into the two
sub-categories of Academy and Foundation members. This
creation of two membership sub-categories was to provide a
class of membership at a lower cost[31] enabling individuals
who met the qualifications, but who could not afford the
previous admission fee and dues, to join the Academy.
Although proposed by the Actors Branch it was "the sentiment
of the Executive Committee of the Board in sponsoring the
amendments that all branches should have the advantage of
the changes proposed."[32]

The first really major revision to the Constitution
and By-Laws occurred in 1933 when the five Branch Executive
Committees were called into an official joint session with
the Board of Directors, and two representatives from each
Branch were appointed to a Constitutional Revision

---

[31]See pages 74 and 76 of this study.

[32]Academy of Motion Picture Arts and Sciences,
Bulletin, No. 28, January 29, 1930, p. 3.

Committee.[33] This major revision was the direct result of the turmoil following Academy involvement in the proposed salary cut discussed in Chapter V, pages 216-219 of this study. Academy members received a copy of their proposal in May of 1933, and in June of 1933 the results of their work were adopted. The most significant changes were as follows: changing the title of the Board of Directors to Board of Governors; replacing the Foundation and Academy categories of membership with one category known as Active; making provisions for the transfer of members between the five branches as desired; provision for the creation of sections within a branch; providing for Awards of Merit; creating the Corporate membership; and changing the requirement for Academy Officers to be elected from the Board of Governors.[34]

Eliminating the two categories of membership known as Foundation and Academy was the solution to an apparent problem which had faced the Board of Directors for the past three years. They had expected acceptance of the lower cost

[33]J. T. Reed, "An Open Letter to Every Member of the Academy," Academy of Motion Picture Arts and Sciences, Bulletin, Vol. 12, May 22, 1933.

[34]Draft of By-Laws, Academy of Motion Picture Arts and Sciences, Bulletin, Vol. 14, June 22, 1933.

type of membership (Academy) only from those who needed to change or apply for that category of membership because of economic factors, and that they would transfer to the other category (Foundation) when possible. By June of 1930 it was apparent that the Board of Directors did not feel the plan was working out since they adopted a resolution against issuing new invitations for the Academy type of membership "except for special reasons." In October of 1930 they changed this to "exceptional reasons," and provided for the Membership Committee to refer all proposals for such membership to the Executive Committee of the respective branch "for investigation and report." The Board of Directors stated that they expected "all members who have been or may be admitted under the Academy member classification will transfer to the Foundation class when and as soon as conditions warrant."[35] A review of the membership records for the three year period showed that there were no significant changes made from Academy to Foundation membership categories; hence the Constitutional Revision Committee recommended abolition of the lower cost sub-category which did not participate fully in Academy

---

[35]Academy of Motion Picture Arts and Sciences, Annual Report, 1930, p. 3.

responsibilities.

The provision for the creation of sections within a branch was initially required because of the different crafts carried under the Technicians Branch. This amendment permitted sections of not less than fifteen members to be formed of persons with like occupations and interests, but such sections were to be governed by the Executive Committee of their parent branch. Five sections were formed within the Technicians Branch: Art Directors, Equipment, Film Editors, Photographic, and Sound.[36] This was the beginning of the formation of new branches in addition to the original five.

The inclusion of regulations related to Awards of Merit within the By-Laws was in recognition of their having become one of the prime working functions of the Academy. In particular the section provided that:

> The Academy shall periodically signalize outstanding achievements in the arts and sciences of motion pictures by the bestowal of Awards of Merit, according to rules to be formulated by a standing Awards Committee, subject to the approval of the Board of Governors. The Awards Committee shall consist of three members from each Branch who shall hold office for three years but with individual terms rotated so there is one new

---

[36]Draft of By-Laws, Academy of Motion Picture Arts and Sciences, Bulletin, Vol. 14, June 22, 1933.

member from each branch each year.[37]

Thus after six years the Academy found it advisable to include in its By-Laws what had originally been stated in the invitation to the organization banquet:

> We can encourage the improvement and the advancement of the arts and sciences of our profession by the interchange of constructive ideas and by awards of merit for distinctive achievements.[38]

The provision for Corporate membership solved two problems. First, it provided a means of financial assistance for the Research Council. Secondly, it provided a place in the Academy structure for those producers who were directly involved with labor matters permitting their participation in Academy affairs while denying them any control over the internal affairs of the Academy. This precaution was necessary to maintain the role of the Academy as an impartial arbiter in labor-management affairs.

The new provision for election of Officers from the entire Academy membership rather than from the Board of Governors was also intended to offset possible criticism. The system of election of Officers from the Board of Governors had originally been designed to provide a continuity

---

[37]Ibid.

[38]Invitation to the Organization Banquet of the Academy of Motion Picture Arts and Sciences, May 11, 1927.

of direct experience in the management operations of the Academy.

However, there is no evidence to demonstrate that either provision of Corporate members or election of Officers from the entire Academy membership had any effect on alleviating criticism or on management effectiveness of the Academy.

The next revisions to the By-Laws occurred in 1937. The Academy now officially withdrew from all labor-management affairs. As expressed by W. S. Van Dyke:

> Now for the first time we are freed of all labor relations responsibility, permitting the Academy to return to its first principles and be non-economic and non-political in theory and in fact.[39]

Thus ended ten years of Academy involvement in labor matters as described in Chapter V, pages 202-226 of this study. Another revision at this time, motivated by declining membership in the Academy, permitted Unions and Guilds to share in the nomination and final voting for the Awards of Merit, thus providing more adequate representation in this function within the profession.

Changes appear in the By-Laws for the Academy dated

---

[39] W. S. Van Dyke, Chairman of the Committee on Reorganization Policy, Academy of Motion Picture Arts and Sciences, "Statement of Policy for Reorganized Academy," 1937.

December 1939 as amended on November 15, 1940. The most
significant changes were: grouping branches into two main
categories, Arts Branches and Science Branches; limiting
the numbers of active members; and designating the five
types of members as Active, Fellow, Foundation, Honorary,
and Life.[40]

Changes to the By-Laws made on January 7, 1941, included the Research Council as a function of the Academy,
redesignated categories for Awards of Merit, and changed
the name of the Producers Branch to Producers and Executives
Branch.[41]

In August of 1943 official branch status was given
to these new categories: Short Subjects, Music, and Public
Relations--thus making eight branches. The By-Laws for
October 1, 1943 also show a revision under Awards of Merit
which limited eligibility to those motion pictures first
publicly exhibited in Los Angeles between January 1 and
midnight December 31 of each calendar year.[42]

---

[40]Academy of Motion Picture Arts and Sciences, By-
Laws dated December, 1939 as amended November 15, 1940.

[41]Academy of Motion Picture Arts and Sciences, By-
Laws dated January 7, 1941.

[42]Academy of Motion Picture Arts and Sciences, By-
Laws dated August, 1943 as amended October 1, 1943.

The Academy By-Laws amended as of December 6, 1946 designate three types of memberships as Active, Honorary, and Life, and list eleven branches as Actors, Art Directors, Cinematographers, Directors, Executives and Producers, Film Editors, Musicians, Public Relations, Short Subjects, Sound, and Writers. Special awards, such as the Irving G. Thalberg Memorial Award, although given before, were now formally provided for under the Awards of Merit in the By-Laws.[43]

By 1946, Academy membership had increased to such an extent that it was again practical to reserve the right of final voting on Awards of Merit to Academy members only; the By-Laws were changed accordingly. The Unions and Guilds were still permitted to participate in the

---

[43]Academy of Motion Picture Arts and Sciences, By-Laws dated December 6, 1946.

Changes after 1947 raised the total of Academy branches to thirteen by separating the Executives and Producers, and adding Administrators; added Associate to membership categories; included Costume Design and Best Picture under Awards of Merit, deleting Best Production; added the Jean Hersholt Humanitarian Award under Special Awards; and provided for an Executive Director and an Assistant Executive Director. These Directors are appointed by the Board of Governors to administer the Academy operations under their guidance, and need not themselves be members of the Academy.

nominations.[44]

Board of Governors

The Board of Governors was originally known as the Board of Directors. The change in title was made in 1933 at the suggestion of a Constitution Revision Committee.[45] Apparently this change was made to reflect more accurately the functions of the Board Members. No record exists of the exact reason for the change, but it did permit use of the word "Director" in later years to designate the Officers of the Academy most directly concerned with day-to-day operations. These Officers are known as Executive Director and Assistant Executive Director, and stemmed from the individual position originally known as the Executive Secretary.

The original number of the Board of Directors was

---

[44]In 1957 both nominations and final voting on Awards was reserved for Academy members. This was just twenty years after the Academy had first requested the Unions and Guilds to actively participate in both the award nomination and final voting. There is no evidence of any favorable or unfavorable reactions to the inclusion and final exclusion of Unions and Guilds in this matter except for a news item in Daily Variety (LIII, No. 3 [September 10, 1946]) to the effect that there was a rush to file membership applications with the Academy following the announcement that final voting would be permitted by Academy members only.

[45]Academy Bulletin, Vol. 12, May 22, 1933, p. 1.

fifteen, with three representatives from each of the five Branches. These first Board members had been selected by the original thirty-six founders from among themselves, and, as stated in the original Constitution and By-Laws, were to "continue in office until the annual election to be held in October, 1927."[46] Thus the original members served a period of five months from May 5, 1927 until the annual election on October 15, 1927.

Four of the original Board members were continued in office at this first annual election. They were Douglas Fairbanks Sr., Milton Sills, and Conrad Nagel from the Actors Branch, and Fred Niblo from the Directors Branch. Information is not available as to why more of the original Board members were not elected. It is quite possible that many of them chose not to be nominated for election having already devoted so much of their time and effort away from their own work. It is also possible that many preferred not to dilute their work for the Academy and lessen the amount of time and effort they could spend with Branch and special committee level activity. It is also possible that some might have believed that it was better for the future

---

[46]Original Constitution and By-Laws adopted May 5, 1927.

of the Academy to have other than just founders on the
Board of Governors. As L. B. Mayer later said: "I suppose
I was very sensitive at one time because I feared some might
say I wanted something out of it."[47] Mary Pickford is said
to have felt that with Douglas Fairbanks Sr. as President
she should not also participate.

To maintain the original policy of ensuring branch
representation on the Board of Governors, it was necessary
to increase the size of the Board as the numbers of the
branches were increased. However, to keep the Board from
becoming unwieldy through sheer numbers, the number of representatives from each branch was reduced to two. Thus by
1947 there were eleven branches and twenty-two members on
the Board of Governors.[48]

To provide for necessary continuity of membership
on the Board the original Constitution and By-Laws added
five new members each year thus making individual service a
matter of three years. To start this system in the beginning, after the first annual election in October of 1927,

---

[47] Academy of Motion Picture Arts and Sciences,
Bulletin, XVI, November 22, 1928, p. 4.

[48] At present (1966) there are thirteen branches and
twenty-six members on the Board of Governors.

the Directors determined by lot which five of them would serve for one year, which for two years, and which for three years.[49]

According to Donald Gledhill, former Executive Secretary of the Academy, the system of providing for staggered terms on the Board worked quite well in providing the necessary continuity of direct knowledge in business affairs permitting operations to proceed smoothly without break. In particular the equal representation from Academy branches provided the kind of collective judgments that were representative of the entire Academy.

Members of the Board of Governors over the years have included such notable figures as B. P. Schulberg, Jack Warner, Douglas Fairbanks Sr., Mary Pickford, Joseph M. Schenck, Milton Sills, Conrad Nagel, Cecil B. de Mille, William C. de Mille, Jean Hersholt, Donald Crisp, J. T. Reed, J. A. Ball, Cedric Gibbons, Waldemar Young, Frank Capra, Johnny Green, Robert Montgomery, Dore Schary, George Stevens, Walter Wanger, Walter Huston, B. B. Kahane, Irving Thalberg, Clark Gable, Darryl Zanuck, and David O. Selznick.

---

[49]Continuity in a like manner is provided for today (1966) by making the term of office for two years, with one new Board member elected from each branch each year.

Physical Location and Facilities
of the Academy

Growth and development of the Academy were marked by
changes in the physical location and facilities. At the
time of its official organization on May 11, 1927 a suite of
offices was rented at 6912 Hollywood Boulevard. Apparently
these offices barely provided room for small committee meetings, and were considered to be merely temporary until the
Academy could work out the means to obtain more suitable
quarters. On June 8, 1927 the Building and Finance Committee submitted a proposal for construction of a new building.
The preliminary sketch was authorized, and the Academy
Secretary instructed to make a survey of the possible ten-
antry that could be expected for excess space within the
building. Plans to build a special building for the Academy
were held in abeyance due to lack of funds.[50]

In November of 1927 the Academy moved to the Roosevelt Hotel at 7010 Hollywood Boulevard. The new quarters,
located on the mezzanine floor, included a club lounge,
anteroom, Board room, business office, and service kitchen.
A complete file of professional periodicals was instituted
for the benefit of the membership, and plans laid to

---

[50]Academy Bulletin, No. 2, June 17, 1927, p. 2.

inaugurate the nucleus of a library.[51] By May of 1928

authority was granted to equip the club lounge with a stan-

dard motion picture projector and screen.[52] On July 16,

1928 the members were informed that projection equipment was

to be installed immediately, providing the most up-to-date

voice and sound reproduction to give members the opportunity

for previews, exhibition of unique pictures, and experimen-

tal testing.[53]

     In November of 1928 it was noted the proper equip-

ment for projecting pictures at the Academy was still not

available due to the tremendous pressure on the manufac-

turers by exhibitors for projection machines which could be

equipped with sound reproduction devices. Appeals were

made directly to the heads of Western Electric and General

Electric pointing out that the Academy served as the only

central clearing house for the purpose of teaching the new

art of sound to the production forces, and would therefore

contribute to the advancement of talking picture quality in

all its branches, technical as well as artistic. This

----

[51]Academy Bulletin, No. 5, November 25, 1927, p. 3.

[52]Academy Bulletin, No. 10, May 3, 1928, p. 4.

[53]Academy Bulletin, No. 11, July 16, 1928, p. 3.

resulted in promises to make the installations by Western
Electric "as speedily as possible," and by General Electric
"as soon after the first of the year as it may be advisable." The equipment was to permit projection of every kind
of sound picture then known--Vitaphone, Movietone, and the
double film process. As Cecil B. de Mille stated: "Every
improvement in the making of sound or talking pictures
should and can be seen here first."[54]

In November of 1928 it was noted that thirty-two
motion picture publications, including several from England,
Canada, France, and Germany, were being kept on file for
the members, and that the skeleton library was being fleshed
out by donations and by some purchases.[55]

Installation of sound reproduction and motion picture projection equipment was finished on April 24, 1929
with the result that the Academy then had one of the most
complete sound and picture reproduction rooms in the West
"barring certain interferences of outside noises."[56]

During 1929 the Academy's library was enlarged and

---

[54]Academy Bulletin, No. XVI, November 22, 1928, p.2.

[55]Ibid.

[56]Annual Report, Academy of Motion Picture Arts and
Sciences, 1929, p. 13.

extended to provide adequate technical references on motion
picture subjects for use by studio employees who were enrolled in the Academy's "School in Fundamentals of Sound
Recording and Reproduction."[57]   A catalogue of the library
was posted in the offices of all principal departments of
the motion picture studios.

On June 1, 1930 the offices of the Academy were
moved from the Roosevelt Hotel to the Professional Building
at 7046 Hollywood Boulevard to provide needed room for the
increased staff, which now consisted of four executives,
three assistants, and six clerks. The Building Committee
was considering a "number of propositions, offering larger
and more adequate quarters, whereby much needed conference
rooms, larger office space, library and projection facilities could be secured."[58]

By the end of 1930 the Academy library was considered to be one of the most complete existing collections of
printed material about motion pictures. It included nearly
all of the then current trade periodicals, as well as

---

[57]Chapter IV of this study provides the details of
this training for studio employees in sound.

[58]Academy of Motion Picture Arts and Sciences,
Annual Report, 1930, p. 28.

reference data and books on the various facets of production. Because of the attention being devoted to the new developments in sound, the library emphasized material on sound recording and reproduction in addition to texts in the related physical and engineering sciences.[59]

In 1935 the Accounting and Executive offices moved to the Taft Building. The library moved to 1455 North Gordon Street, where the Players' Directory[60] was located in 1937.

In 1936, with the acquisition of a full-time professional librarian, the Academy library began a fully professional approach, including a complete cataloguing system. A listing of the books in the Academy library was sent to 300 leading libraries with the request that it be checked against their holdings, and returned to the Academy with a list of their books in the field of motion pictures which were not on the Academy listing. About 20 percent of the libraries responded, and these lists were compiled as a basis for expanding the Academy library. These lists were further supplemented with all Library of Congress cards on

---

[59] Ibid., p. 24.

[60] The Players' Directory is discussed on page 62 of this study.

motion pictures. The Academy already held 90 percent of all the books listed by other libraries; steps were taken to obtain the lacking 10 percent. The Academy library thus progressed from a valuable reference source to becoming the authoritative source of information about the field of motion pictures.[61]

By 1940 the Academy had continued to expand its specialized library on all phases of motion pictures until it ranked among the top of its kind in the world.[62] By 1941 the archival and reference library of the Academy had attained full stature as one of the three most complete collections in the specialized field of motion pictures.[63] Historical data, statistics, photographs, and production information extended from 1896 to 1941. Rapid growth of the library and available literature was indicated by the addition of 260 books during the year. In addition some 250 selected motion picture scripts, 90 bound volumes of both U. S. and foreign trade magazines, plus several thousand

---

[61] Pacific Bindery Talk, XIII, No. 2 (October, 1940).

[62] Donald Gledhill, "The Motion Picture Academy, a Cooperative in Hollywood," The Journal of Educational Sociology, XIII, No. 5 (January, 1940), p. 271.

[63] The other two collections were those of the Museum of Modern Art, and the New York Public Library.

still photographs were added to the library. The library
was now considered to include nearly all the books ever published in any language about motion pictures. A file of
production information on nearly 20,000 motion pictures produced since 1900, still photographs from the 1,000 most important films produced since 1915, and scripts from the most
significant productions since 1925 were now contained in the
library.[64]

By 1943 the library had established a special library of 275 war films of Great Britain, Canada, Russia,
Mexico, and the United States. It had also established a
special clipping file dealing with the effects of the war
on the motion picture industry.[65]

In 1946 the Academy purchased a twenty-five year
old theatre building, then called the Marquis Theatre, from
the Fox West Coast Theatres and renamed it the Academy
Award Theatre. The auditorium seated just under 1,000
people. Modifications in accordance with a redesign by the
Academy Research Council resulted in an auditorium as

---

[64]Annual Report, Academy of Motion Picture Arts and
Sciences, 1941, pp. 2-3.

[65]"A Report--The Academy in Wartime," Academy of
Motion Picture Arts and Sciences, May 1, 1943.

nearly acoustically perfect as any in existence. By August
of 1946 all Academy functions had moved into the theatre
building, pulling together the Accounting and Executive
offices, Players' Directory staff, and library under one
roof. The library now had adequate shelving for its 2,500
volume collection, and was further expanded by the addition
of 95 reels of very early silent films.[66] By 1947 the library was well settled and furnishing expanded services.[67]

Publications of the Academy

The Academy issues, for internal administrative purposes only, an annual report and a series of informational
notices to members, originally known as Academy Bulletins
and now as News Letters. The Academy, on three different
occasions, attempted to sponsor its own magazine. The first
attempt was made in 1927 with a magazine called Motion

---

[66]Report of the President, 1945-1947, Academy of
Motion Picture Arts and Sciences.

[67]At the present time (1966) the Academy library
contains over 5,000 volumes on motion pictures and related
subjects. It subscribes to over fifty periodicals related
to the motion picture industry, and has a file of trade
journals dating back in some cases to 1906. The film library is primarily for archival storage rather than viewing,
as in the case of the Library of Congress holdings on
paper-print materials which were all converted to 16mm
safety film by 1964.

Picture Arts and Sciences, the second time in 1928 with a magazine called Hollywood, and the third time in 1939 with a magazine called Montage.

Motion Picture Arts and Sciences was edited by Carey Wilson, Cedric Gibbons, and Waldemar Young. It was printed by Yount and McCallister, Incorporated, in Los Angeles. Only one issue was ever published and circulated to the membership of the Academy--early in November of 1927. It was intended to appeal only to the motion picture production profession, and not for general circulation.

In 1928 the Board of Directors considered the purchase of a magazine called Hollywood.[68] After some five months of careful deliberation the Board took an option, in December of 1928, for purchase of the magazine one year from the date of the contract. In April of 1929, just five months later, the contract was "cancelled by mutual consent and without prejudice." The Director's statement went on to say:

> The plan appeared to be an excellent one if prac-
> ticable. As matters worked out, however, the terms
> of the contract operated to prevent the free develop-
> ment of the magazine as a national publication. As
> a periodical of limited circulation could be of no
> great value to the Academy, it was felt by both the

[68]Academy Bulletin, XVI, November 22, 1928, p. 13.

publisher and the Board of Directors of the Academy that the experiment should be discontinued.[69]

Montage was actually an idea, set aside because of World War II, to resurrect the magazine Motion Picture Arts and Sciences under a new title and format. One experimental issue was printed in 1939, and for a time the Board of Governors considered continuous publication. The Executive Secretary of the Academy, in an article for The Journal of Education Sociology, stated:

> During the coming year, conditional upon the effects of the war, a new service is planned of direct interest to educators. This will be the monthly publication of an Academy magazine under the title of "Montage," primarily for the industry, but available to the public by subscription, and providing news, commentary, and authoritative reference material about motion pictures upon a level comparable to the academic and professional journals in other fields.[70]

The Academy's first publication was entitled Report on Incandescent Illumination, and was the complete record of the investigations and demonstrations conducted by the Academy during the months of January, February, March, and April of 1928 concerning incandescent and arc illumination. Copies of this publication were placed in the reference libraries of several universities, and the research

---

[69]Academy Bulletin, No. XX, April 8, 1929, p. 5.

[70]Gledhill, loc. cit.

departments of General Electric, Western Electric, Bell
Telephone, Westinghouse, Bell & Howell, Eastman Kodak,
DuPont, and Bausch & Lomb. It was also ordered by such
foreign countries as England, Germany, Switzerland, China,
and India.[71]

Technical Bulletins were issued by the Research
Council of the Academy at indeterminate intervals as pro-
jects and studies were completed by the working committees:
for example, "Theatre Acoustics for Reproduced Sound, also
Reproduction in the Theatre," "Camera Silencing Devices,"
"A Selected Glossary for the Motion Picture Technician,"
"Architectural Acoustics," and "Methods of Silencing Arcs."

In 1929 the Academy and the University of Southern
California jointly copyrighted a mimeographed publication
entitled "Introduction to the Photoplay" based upon the lectures given during the course in Photoplay given that year
at the University of Southern California as covered in
Chapter IV, pages 110-114 of this study.

In 1933 the Academy started publication of three
credit bulletins called the Writers' Bulletin, the Directors' Bulletin, and the Production List. An annual

---

[71]Academy of Motion Picture Arts and Sciences,
Bulletin, XVI, November 22, 1928, p. 11.

cumulative volume was first issued in 1938 with monthly
supplements to keep the records up to date. Distributed by
subscription service primarily to studios and production
units it came to be known as the Bulletin of Screen Achievement Records.[72]

The Players' Directory Bulletin was first published
in 1937, and was a casting directory. Issue Number 4, dated
September, 1937, shows the name changed to The Academy
Players Directory. Continually published since 1937, it is
maintained as a cooperative service for the players and
studios. By 1941 more than 1800 actors and actresses were
listed in this publication, and subscriptions costs were becoming excessive. Therefore, at the request of the Screen
Actors Guild the frequency of issue was reduced to three
times a year. The initiative in 1937 for publishing such a
directory came from the Executive Secretary of the Academy.
In 1940 he wrote:

> In a direct way the Academy has saved motion picture
> actors and actresses thousands of dollars during the
> past three years. Previously Hollywood was overrun
> with private "casting directories"--publications con-
> taining the photographs and credits of players. These
> were commercially exploited, and prices kept beyond
> the means of the lower paid actors. In 1937 the

---

[72]Annual Report, Academy of Motion Picture Arts and
Sciences, 1941, pp. 1-2.

Academy established a unified players directory service
to end all such racketeering. In this publication all
names are treated alike, with the biggest star allowed
no larger photograph or more space than the most minor
"bit" player.[73]

The Academy's next publication effort was based
upon lectures given during the Academy's course in sound
fundamentals.[74] These lectures had been published as individual papers in the Academy Technical Bulletins. However,
the Board of Directors decided the papers should be published in book form, and thus be "made available to all
creative workers and technicians in studios, laboratories,
and theatres as a common textbook to promote that mutual
understanding and coordination which is vital to the growth
of the industry."[75]

Published in 1931 the final text consisted of these
papers expanded and revised by the lecturers, and was entitled Recording Sound for Motion Pictures. A review of the
contents reveals that it was the most comprehensive single
reference source on all current sound recording practices
then used in the motion picture industry.

---

[73]Gledhill, loc. cit.

[74]See Chapter IV, pp. 132-135, of this study for
details on the sound course.

[75]Lester Cowan (ed.), Recording Sound for Motion
Pictures (New York: McGraw-Hill Book Company, Inc., 1931),
p. vii.

In the first section of the text, H. G. Knox, Vice
President of Electrical Research Products, Incorporated,[76]
briefly provided the history of sound including the discov-
eries of Edison, Bell, Marconi, and DeForest. He highlight-
ed the impact of the film Don Juan which had been produced
in 1926, the first Movietone newsreel produced in 1927, and
the film The Jazz Singer, which was also produced in 1927.
Noting that there were 16 recording channels in use in
Hollywood by the end of 1928, Knox pointed out that these
had increased to 116 by the end of 1929. Knox believed the
writers, producers, directors, and actors were already becoming conversant with the possibilities and techniques of
sound, and that soon the "loosening shackles of the machine
will be completely thrown off" so that "film dialogue,
music, dramatic silence and effects will combine to make an
imaginative and enduring tale."[77] A. W. Nye, Professor of
Physics at the University of Southern California, provided
a chapter on the nature of sound.

The balance of the text was broken into four major
sections covering sound recording equipment, film, studio

[76]Electrical Research Products, Inc., was a market-
ing subsidiary of Western Electric.

[77]Cowan (ed.), op. cit., p. 12.

acoustics and technique, and sound reproduction. The first

section on sound recording equipment included information on

disc recording for Vitaphone, recording on film for Fox

Movietone, the theory and operation of transmission circuits,

sound dubbing, and accessory and special equipment. The

second section on film included data from Eastman Kodak on

film used as a sound recording medium, the photographic re-

quirements of variable density recording, laboratory tech-

niques for sound pictures, and techniques involved in the

editing and assembling of a sound film. The third section

on studio acoustics and techniques included data on sound

stages, sound recording practices, and acoustics. The

fourth section dealt with sound reproduction in theatres and

included the practice and problems of sound projection.

Recording Sound for Motion Pictures proved the value

of the cooperative effort achieved by the technical activi-

ties of the Academy in working with studio, commercial, and

University personnel.

The development of equipment and techniques for

sound recording in motion pictures was to advance very

rapidly from 1931 through 1936. As outlined in Chapter IV,

pages 136-137 of this study, the Research Council of the

Academy provided a new series of courses in sound during

the fall of 1936 and the spring of 1937 for all interested
personnel in the motion picture industry. Gordon S.
Mitchell, Manager of the Academy Research Council, decided
that a new book about sound should be published for the
benefit of the industry which would be based on this latest
series of lectures.[78] Under his leadership the new book
Motion Picture Sound Engineering[79] was prepared and published in 1938.

The first part of the new book consisted of twenty-
four chapters all based on the advanced course in sound except for three chapters on film drive, re-recording for release, and the basis of motion picture sound. These three
chapters, by Wesley C. Miller and Kenneth Lambert of Metro-
Goldwyn-Mayer Studios, were added to provide complete cov-
erage on the subject of motion picture sound recording and
reproducing. The chapter on the basis of motion picture
sound established the role of the sound technician as an
individual who must maintain achieved quality but work towards giving greater freedom to the creative film producer.

---

[78]Gordon S. Mitchell. Personal correspondence,
January 19, 1966.
[79]Research Council of the Academy of Motion Picture
Arts and Sciences, Motion Picture Sound Engineering (New
York: D. Van Nostrand Company, Inc., 1938).

L. E. Clark, of RCA, provided three chapters on the nature
of sound, microphones, and film processing. John Hilliard,
of Metro-Goldwyn-Mayer Studios, provided four chapters on
sound circuits, measurements in sound circuits, phase dis-
tortion, and transformers for sound circuits. Clark and
Hilliard wrote three chapters on the types of film recording, headphones and loud-speakers, and reproducing systems.
Fred Albin, of United Artists Studios, wrote five chapters
on noise reduction, vacuum tube amplifier circuits, recti-
fiers, and volume indicators. Harry Kimball, of Metro-
Goldwyn-Mayer Studios, prepared six chapters on general
network theory, attenuation equalizers, equalizer design,
wave filter theory, low-pass and high-pass filters, and
dividing networks for loud-speakers.

A. P. Hill, of Electrical Research Products, Incorporated, who had conducted the preliminary courses in
sound, prepared the second part of the book which consisted
of fifteen short chapters dealing with such basic subjects
as direct and alternating currents, static electricity,
generators and motors, resonant circuits, static electricity
and triode amplifiers.

Recording Sound for Motion Pictures and Motion
Picture Sound Engineering, having been based on training

lectures, presented their subject matter in clear and con-
cise terms. Both books were well received in the motion
picture industry and used extensively.[80]

Membership

Charter membership was offered to the 300 men and
women who had been invited to the organization banquet on
May 11, 1927 by the founders. Of these, 231 accepted membership on that evening of the banquet.[81]

From the very beginning of the Academy there was
no attempt made at any form of a membership drive. Individuals at the organization banquet, who had been designated
by Levee[82] to take the names of parties interested in becoming members, had been specifically instructed "not to solic-
it anybody at any table, that this proposition was one of
invitation and free decision as to membership."[83] This
basic principle of membership by invitation only and individual choice in acceptance rather than any form of

---

[80]Mitchell, loc. cit.

[81]Annual Report, Academy of Motion Picture Arts and
Sciences, 1929, p. 58.

[82]Levee, loc. cit.

[83]Academy Bulletin, No. XVI, November 22, 1928, p.4.

solicitation has been adhered to over the years.

As indicated in June of 1927:

Membership in the Academy has increased steadily, since
the organization dinner, despite the fact that there
has not been and will not be any attempt to conduct a
"drive." Membership in the Academy is by invitation
only, and should be considered a recognition of distinctive service to the profession.[84]

As indicated in September of 1929:

Qualification for membership is based on distinctive
achievements in the different branches of motion picture production. It has never been the policy of
the Academy to conduct campaigns for membership and
all increase of enrollment is therefore indicative
of normal healthy advancement.[85]

By the time of the annual meeting of the Academy

on November 3, 1928 the membership had reached 374. Most

significantly, it now included Mr. Sinclair-Hill who was

the Managing Director and Chief Producer of Stoll Picture

Productions, Ltd., London, England. The addition of

Sinclair-Hill pointed to the fact that the Academy was

thought of in the beginning as an international institu-

tion.[86]

---

[84]Academy Bulletin, No. 2, June 17, 1927, p. 2.

[85]Academy Bulletin, No. XXV, September 25, 1929,
p. 4.

[86]Academy Bulletin, No. XVI, November 22, 1928,
p. 13.

It must be remembered, however, that Academy facilities and functions have always been located in Hollywood
which has been the center of world film production. As a
natural consequence, the membership and character of the
organization have been predominantly American.

A survey of membership reveals a steady increase in
members to over 800 by 1932. After the bank-crisis period
in 1933 as covered in Chapter V, pages 216-219 of this
study, there was a gradual decline, particularly of actors
and writers, through the late thirties to the 1929 level of
over 400 members. Then began an increase until by 1947
there were 1650 members.[87]

The classification of Active Member has always been
assigned to members who had full rights and privileges of
the Academy. However, in 1930, at the request of the Actors
Branch, it was deemed advisable to permit the admission of
active members under some classification that would not
call for the standard admission fee of $100 and dues of
$5.00 per month, but for the lesser amounts of $15.00 for
admission and dues of $1.00. This divided the Active mem-
ber classification into two categories known as Academy

---

[87]Membership records of the Academy of Motion
Picture Arts and Sciences.

TABLE 1

PATTERN OF MEMBERSHIP CATEGORIES IN THE ACADEMY OF
MOTION PICTURE ARTS AND SCIENCES (1927-1946) [a]

1927	1930	1933	1940	1946
Active	Active [b]	Active	Active	Active
Associate	Associate	Associate	. . .	. . .
Honorary	Honorary	Honorary	Honorary	Honorary
Special	Special	Special	. . .	. . .
. . .	. . .	Life	Life	Life
. . .	. . .	Corporate	. . .	. . .
. . .	. . .	. . .	Foundation	. . .
. . .	. . .	. . .	Fellow	. . .

[a]Present (1966) categories of members are Active, Associate, and
Members-at-Large.

[b]The Active members for 1930 were split into two further categories of
"Academy" and "Foundation."

members who would pay the lesser amount and Foundation members who had paid or would pay the larger amounts. Academy
members were entitled to all rights and privileges except
those of serving on the Board of Directors or holding
offices in the government of the Academy as a whole. Members from either the Academy classification or Foundation
classification were eligible to transfer from one to the
other.[88] This division of Active members was eliminated
with the revised By-Laws in 1933.

The category of Associate member was provided for
in the original Constitution and By-Laws as:

> Any person who is engaged in any of those production
> branches of the motion picture industry hereinafter
> mentioned in Section 5 of this article (Actors, Direc-
> tors, Producers including executives of producing
> organizations, Technicians, and Writers), who is of
> good moral and personal standing, may become an asso-
> ciate member of the Academy, by vote of the board of
> directors, on recommendation of the committee on
> membership, and on paying the dues for the current
> month, including any original admission fee.[89]

Honorary membership was provided for in the original Constitution and By-Laws as:

Any person distinguished for public service or

---

[88]Academy Bulletin, No. XXIX, February 27, 1930,
p. 6.

[89]Academy Constitution and By-Laws as adopted May
5, 1927.

eminence in the motion picture industry, or by
reason of any contribution made thereto, may, by
the unanimous vote of the board of directors, become
an honorary member of the Academy, without the payment of dues, and with all the privileges except that
of voting. Not more than five (5) persons shall be
elected honorary members during any calendar year.[90]

The first person to be given an Honorary membership
by the Academy was Thomas A. Edison. Tribute was paid to
Mr. Edison at the organization banquet held on May 11, 1927.
He responded by letter to the President of the Academy
stating:

> I wish you would kindly convey to the Academy my
> appreciation of the high honor they have done me
> by the tribute which you state was their first
> official act.[91]

Upon receipt of the framed scroll of Honorary Membership Mr. Edison wrote to the Academy:

> I have been the happy recipient of a framed scroll
> bearing an invitation to me to accept the distinc-
> tion of being the First Honorary Member of the
> Academy of Motion Picture Arts and Sciences.
>
> Allow me to express my keen appreciation of this
> pleasant manifestation of the high regard in which
> you hold me, and please receive this letter as my
> grateful acceptance of the distinguished honor you
> have conferred upon me.

---

[90]Ibid.

[91]Letter from Thomas A. Edison to the President of
the Academy of Motion Picture Arts and Sciences, Bulletin,
No. 2, June 17, 1927, Academy of Motion Picture Arts and
Sciences.

> The scroll itself is unique and interesting and
> will occupy a prominent place in the library at my
> laboratory. It will be a treasured possession as
> it contains the signatures, not only of many of my
> old friends, but also of the many who have contributed
> to the pleasure of the world by their artistic work
> on the screen.[92]

As a further token of his sincere appreciation of the honor paid to him by the Academy, Edison sent a talking picture reel of film to the Academy for its fourth annual meeting on November 5, 1930.[93] In this film Mr. Edison again thanked the Academy for the honor of being the first Honorary member. The text of Edison's remarks are given in Appendix III of this study. The reel of film was projected by means of a portable sound and picture reproducing machine provided by the Electrical Research Products, Incorporated.

The second Honorary member was George Eastman who was elected in 1930. Eastman sent a message of acceptance and gratitude to the Academy as follows:

> Will you kindly convey to the Board of Directors
> of the Academy of Motion Picture Arts and Sciences
> my appreciation for the honor which they have done

---

[92]Letter from Thomas A. Edison to the President of the Academy of Motion Picture Arts and Sciences, Annual Report of the President of the Academy, 1930.

[93]Annual Report, Academy of Motion Picture Arts and Sciences, 1930, p. 2.

me in inviting me to become an honorary member of
the Academy and tell them that it gives me great
pleasure to accept their invitation. I am familiar
with the work the Academy is doing in the industry
and I am very glad indeed to have my name associated
with it.[94]

The category of Special member was provided for in

the original Constitution and By-Laws as:

Any person not included in any of the classes or
branches hereinafter specified, in Section 5 of this
article, but actively engaged or connected with the
motion picture industry, may become a special member
of the Academy, by vote of the board of directors,
on recommendation of the committee on membership, and
on paying the dues for the current month, including
any original admission fees. Special members shall
not be entitled to vote or hold office.[95]

The category of Life member was provided for in the

change of the By-Laws in 1933 as:

Any member of the Academy unusually distinguished
for service to the motion picture industry through
leadership in the activities of the Academy may by
vote of 2/3rds of all Governors, become a Life member of the Academy, without the payment of dues.
Life members shall have all of the voting and office-
holding privileges of Active members of the branch
to which they belong; and whenever language is used
in these By-Laws conferring any such privileges upon
Active members, such language shall include and be
deemed to include Life members, unless Life members
are therein expressly excepted.[96]

---

[94]Ibid., p. 1.

[95]Academy Constitution and By-Laws as adopted
May 5, 1927.

[96]By-Laws of the Academy, June 22, 1933.

In December of 1946 the By-Laws were amended to automatically include all past Presidents of the Academy as Life members.[97]

The Corporate member appeared in the 1933 draft of
the new By-Laws replacing the original Constitution and By-
Laws as:

> Any corporation or firm within the motion picture
> industry may become a Corporate member of the Academy
> by vote of the Board of Governors on subscribing to
> or agreeing to be bound by all Academy pacts, agree-
> ments and codes in force at the time of admission
> and prescribed by said Board for such Corporate mem-
> bership. Corporate members shall not be eligible to
> vote nor to participate in the internal affairs of
> any Branch or of the Academy as a whole but may be
> represented on the Research Council. Fees are to be
> used solely for approved purposes of the Research
> Council.[98]

The purpose of creating the Corporate membership was to
provide the means for financial assistance to the Research
Council of the Academy, and uniformity of cooperative effort on the part of the industries in working under Academy
auspices for the technical advancement of motion pictures.
This category of membership was discontinued in the By-Laws
of November 15, 1940.

The category of Foundation member was created by

---

[97] By-Laws of the Academy, December 6, 1946.

[98] By-Laws of the Academy, June 22, 1933.

the new By-Laws of November 15, 1940 to provide a mechanism

for the financial support of special projects, such as the

building of a museum,[99] which would be beyond the capabili-

ties of a treasury relying solely on the dues of individ-

uals.

The category of Fellow was established to confer a

type of membership on all those who were winners of Awards

of Merit. However, in actual practice any nominee was in-

vited to become an active member so this category was not

used.

Officers

The original Constitution and By-Laws named the

officers of the Academy as the President, Vice-President,

Treasurer, Secretary, fifteen Directors, and twenty-five

Executive Committeemen. The Directors have been discussed

under the section of this chapter, pages 51-54, devoted to

the Board of Governors. The Presidents have included such

outstanding figures in the motion picture industry as

Douglas Fairbanks Sr., William C. de Mille, Frank Capra,

Jean Hersholt, George Seaton, and George Stevens.

From the Academy founding date in 1927 until August

---

[99]By-Laws of the Academy, November 15, 1940.

of 1933 the President and Vice President were required to be members of the Board of Directors. From August of 1933 until December of 1940 a second Vice President was added to the officers, and officers not already members of the Board became so upon election to office.[100] From January 1941 until May of 1948 a third and fourth Vice President were added together with an Assistant Secretary and an Assistant Treasurer. Officers, upon election, became members of the Board of Governors until August of 1946 when all officers were elected from the Board of Governors.[101]

Branches

The original concept of the Academy was that of an organization uniting all main facets of motion picture production. Thus the Academy was first organized into five branches: Actors, Directors, Writers, Producers, and Technicians. The branches have always been autonomous

---

[100]As covered on page 47 of this study, this was primarily to offset criticism that election of officers only from the Board of Governors appeared to limit control to a select few. Actually election from the Board had been intended to provide a continuity in the understanding and execution of Academy programs.

[101]After 1948 the number of officers was reduced to a President, first and second Vice President, Secretary, Assistant Secretary, Treasurer, and Assistant Treasurer.

groups who met as necessary to deal with their separate problems. They remained subject to the Academy's Constitution and By-Laws, but each had its own officials and representatives on the Board of Directors of the Academy.

As the motion picture industry grew in complexity the number of Academy branches was increased to insure continued representation from all major facets of production. Thus by 1947 there were twelve branches: Actors, Art Directors, Directors, Cinematographers, Executive, Producers, Film Editors, Music, Public Relations, Short Subjects, Sound, and Writers.

The first evidence of this growth was the establishment of five sections within the Technicians branch in 1931: Art Directors, Equipment, Film Editors, Photographic, and Sound. The revised Academy By-Laws of 1933 authorized the Board of Governors to create sections within a branch at the request of the Executive Committee of that branch, thus legalizing actions already taken by the Technicians branch. Each section so created consisted of no less than 15 members, and had to be governed and conducted according to rules prescribed by the Executive Committee of the branch to which the section belonged.[102]

By 1941 there were a total of eleven branches, grouped into the Arts Branches and the Science Branches. The Arts Branches included Actors, Directors, Producers and Executives, Writers, Music, Short Subjects, and Publicity Directors. The Science Branches included Art Direction, Photographic, Sound, and Film Editors. Memberships in the Actors, Directors, Writers, and Producers branches were limited to 150 each; in the Music, Short Subjects, and Public Relations branches to not more than 50 in each branch. At this time the total membership of the Academy was limited to 1,000 active members.[103] In 1947 the number of branches was increased to twelve by division of the Producers and Executives into separate branches.

Technical Activities

The many technical activities of the Academy were always for the benefit of the entire motion picture industry.[104] They began under various special committees individually created for particular areas of concern; as, for

---

[102]By-Laws of the Academy, June 22, 1933.

[103]By-Laws of the Academy, November 15, 1940.

[104]Mitchell, loc. cit.

example, the Screen Illumination Committee, the Aperture

Committee, and the Committee on Coordination of Release

Prints for Theatres.

In 1929 the Producers-Technicians Joint Committee

was formed in order to group the various technical activi-

ties of the Academy under a central control. The Committee

was the outgrowth of a meeting on July 31 between the Pro-

ducers Branch of the Academy and executives from various

studios. Two actions were recommended to the Academy Board

of Directors as a result of this meeting: (1) to establish

a school for studio personnel to teach the elements of

sound recording and reproduction, and (2) to establish a

Producers-Technicians Joint Committee to provide central

and responsible direction of the handling of specific prob-

lems that would benefit from cooperative research, investi-

gation, and experimentation.[105]

The Producers-Technicians Joint Committee[106] held

its first meeting on November 12, 1929 and adopted a policy

---

[105]Annual Report, Academy of Motion Picture Arts
and Sciences, 1929, p. 49.

[106]The members were Irving Thalberg, M. C. Levee,
Fred W. Beetson, J. A. Ball, Fred Pelton, J. T. Reed,
Gerald Rackett, Sol Wurtzel, William Sistrom, Walter Stern,
H. Keith Weeks, and Nugent H. Slaughter.

of concentrating on problems of immediate practical significance. The Committee recommended to the Academy Board of
Directors that efforts be concentrated initially on three
problems, namely: (1) silencing the camera, (2) developing
special set construction materials for sound pictures, and
(3) silencing the arc. These and subsequent problems were
assigned to sub-committees appointed from Joint Committee
membership. This membership was reappointed annually by
the President of the Academy on the recommendations of the
Executive Committees of the Producers and Technicians
branches.

The operations of the Joint Committee increasingly
paralleled those of the Technical Bureau of the Association
of Motion Picture Producers and the cooperation between the
two groups became very close. In January of 1930 the Association transferred its Technical Bureau to the Academy together with an annual appropriation for its support. The
Joint Committee work had been supported by Academy membership dues.[107] With the transfer of the Technical Bureau
to the Academy its work was then consolidated with that of
the Producers-Technicians Joint Committee.

---

[107]Mitchell, loc. cit.

The theme for their cooperative effort was expressed in the following statement:

> Motion pictures may be called an art existing by grace of mechanics, but it is the art and not the mechanics that is sold to the public. Studios all need good cameras for instance, but the only use of a camera is to photograph a scene. It is the value of the scene which will be in competition with the product of other studios. If every camera could be made twice as efficient, the competition would remain the same, but the industry as a whole would benefit and every studio in proportion.[108]

The Research Council of the Academy of Motion Picture Arts and Sciences was established by the Board of Directors in 1932 to coordinate all technical and investigational activities of the organization under one governing body. In addition to work done under the Technical Bureau, and before that the Producers-Technicians Joint Committee, there had been certain projects handled by special committees such as the Art and Technique Committee. The Research Council assumed full responsibility for all such technical efforts. It consisted of representatives from the five branches of the Academy, and a technical representative from each of the major producing organizations. Each of the principal equipment and manufacturing companies which

---

[108]Academy of Motion Picture Arts and Sciences, Technical Bureau Bulletin, July 15, 1930.

dealt with the motion picture industry appointed an engineering executive to represent the company on the Research Council in an advisory capacity.

The first meeting of the Research Council was held on August 15, 1932, and it met quarterly thereafter. The work was carried on by subcommittees, each appointed to deal with one specific project. Although the subcommittees were composed of experts in a particular field, representatives from other fields were called upon for counsel and cooperation as some problems required this.[109] There were eight cooperative projects in the hands of separate committees in 1934. That same year Jack Alicoate commented that "in the matter of recorded cooperative technical and artistic advancement, the Academy stands alone."[110] He added that "its program of standardization saved millions for the industry, and that it provides a common meeting ground for those with like problems."[111] Beginning in March of 1934 monthly contributions from various studios financed the

[109] Academy of Motion Picture Arts and Sciences, Research Council Technical Bulletin Supplement, No. 15, November 15, 1932, p. 1.

[110] Jack Alicoate, news item in Film Daily, LXV, No. 41 (February 19, 1934).

[111] Ibid.

Research Council activities.[112]

There were thirty-six technical committees by 1938 investigating problems of sound recording, sound reproduction, projection, laboratory practices, film preservation, photography, set acoustics, and lighting. The Research Council demonstrated its value to the profession in those pre-war years, and during wartime the existence of such a proven organization was invaluable to the national interest. It was natural to turn to such a group for specialized training of military personnel, production of training films, recommendations of specialized photographic personnel for duty in the military, and for the solutions to specialized military equipment problems. The changes in tempo and viewpoint engendered by wartime activities made it impossible to go back to pre-war patterns; the last major project of the Research Council as an Academy organization was the acoustic redesign of the Academy theatre which was completed in 1947. The exponential increase in research and development in post-war years affected the motion picture profession as radically as any. The Academy had nurtured and developed the Research Council, but the

---

[112]Mitchell, loc. cit.

research requirements of the industry were now of a tempo
and scope inappropriate to the basic Academy structure.[113]

Awards of Merit

The invitation to the Organization Banquet of the
Academy stated:

> We can encourage the improvement and advancement of
> the arts and sciences of our profession by the inter-
> change of constructive ideas and by awards of merit
> for distinctive achievements.[114]

This particular function of the Academy membership
in bestowing Awards of Merit on their peers was to achieve
and retain world-wide interest. Despite the extensive publicity given to this particular function of the Academy, it
is desirable to review some of the more pertinent aspects
as they developed up to 1947.

In 1927 a committee to formulate an award program

---

[113]Subsequent to the cut-off date of this study, in
January of 1948, the Academy Research Council became the
Motion Picture Research Council under the Producers Association. In so doing it could accept funds directly from
commercial companies for an expanded technical program, and
could enter into commercial negotiations and apply for and
obtain patents for the benefit of the studios. Although
this move separated the Research Council from the Academy
it did not affect the status of the individual Research
Council members in the Academy.

[114]Invitation to the Organization Banquet of the
Academy of Motion Picture Arts and Sciences, May 11, 1927.

was established with the following members: Chairman,
Cedric Gibbons, Sid Grauman, Bess Meredith, J. Stuart Blackton, Richard Barthelmess, Henry King, and D. W. Griffith.
The awards program as conceived by this group was to change
in details over the years but has always adhered to the basic concept of awards given for achievement of outstanding
creativity as evaluated by a group of proven ability in the
same field.

Cedric Gibbons originated the basic idea for the
trophy to be given for first place awards. George Stanley,
a prominent Los Angeles sculptor, modeled the figure after
it was approved by the Academy Board of Directors.[115] The

---

[115]According to Academy records, this statuette was
named "Oscar" by the present Executive Director of the Academy, Margaret Herrick, and is recognized the world over by
that name. However, it is alleged by others that the name
"Oscar" was given to the statuette by writer Sidney Skol-
sky, publicity director John LeRoy Johnston, or actress
Bette Davis. It is the official trophy for all Annual
Awards, the Documentary Awards, the Jean Hersholt Humanitarian Award, and Class I Scientific or Technical Awards. The
Honorary Juvenile Award is a miniature statuette; the Class
II Scientific or Technical Awards receive a plaque, and
Class III Scientific or Technical Awards receive a Certifi-
cate of Honorable Mention. The Irving G. Thalberg Memorial
Award is a bronze head of Mr. Thalberg. Except as specified
all Honorary Awards may take the form of a statuette, a Life
membership, a scroll or any other design indicated by the
Board of Governors. For example, a wood statuette was
awarded to Edgar Bergen at the 10th Awards in 1937.

figure stands 13 1/2 inches tall, weighs 6 3/4 pounds, and
is made of gold plated britannium. It represents a knight
holding a crusader's sword, and stands on a film reel with
five spokes representing the five original branches of the
Academy.

The first awards (1927-1928) bestowed by Academy
membership were for motion pictures which had been released
in Los Angeles between August 1, 1927 and July 31, 1928.
These awards were determined by nominations of Academy members, reviewed by Boards of Judges representing the five
branches, and finally decided by a central board of Judges
consisting of one representative from each branch. This
system went through four changes between 1927 and 1947.
The first change, effective for the third annual awards
(1929-1930), relegated both nominations and final vote to
the general membership. The second change, effective for
the ninth annual awards (1936), required that nominations
originate from an Awards Nominating Committee appointed by
the President of the Academy. This Committee had equal representation from each branch. Final voting for the awards
was by Academy membership. The third change, effective for
the tenth annual awards (1937), gave the members of the
guilds and unions equal status with members of the Academy

in the selection process. Both nominations and final vote
were relegated to the general memberships of guilds, unions,
and the Academy. The fourth change, effective for the nineteenth annual awards (1946), permitted nominations by Academy membership and the guilds and unions, but reserved final vote to the Academy membership only.[116]

According to Donald Gledhill, Executive Secretary
of the Academy during this period in 1937, the participation of guilds and unions in Award nominations and final
voting was not considered to be a momentous event in the
motion picture industry. By that date membership in the
Academy, particularly in the Actors' Branch and Writers'
Branch, had declined with the interest in developing guilds
and unions so that it became desirable to go outside the
Academy to obtain additional numbers to make the Awards
truly representative of the motion picture industry. This
arrangement was accomplished by an informal conversation
between Donald Gledhill, the Academy Executive Secretary,
and Ken Thompson, Manager of the Screen Actors' Guild. The
Academy took the initiative of asking the Guild to address

---

[116]This system applied through the twenty-ninth
Annual Awards (1956). From the thirtieth Annual Awards
(1957) through to the present (1966) both nominations and
final voting has been by Academy membership only.

Awards ballots to its own membership, and made similar requests to other union organizations simply to avoid charges
of discrimination or inadequate representation. The unions
and guilds watched each other closely to make sure that one
did not have an advantage over another. For example, in
1938 the Academy had to correct the situation after the
Screen Playwrights protested that the Screen Writers' Guild
was more favored in the matter of representation on nominating committees.[117] The privilege of the final vote was
taken back into the Academy[118] in 1946 when the membership
had increased to over a thousand.[119]

By the ninth Annual Awards (1936), the preferential
system of voting in nominations was introduced and has been
used since that time.

The preferential system of voting is described by
the Academy as follows:

Under the preferential system of voting, each member
has one vote, which may be expressed in several
alternate choices, in the order of his preference.

[117]News item in New York Times, January 27, 1938.

[118]News item in Daily Variety, LIII, No. 54 (August
21, 1946).

[119]News item in Daily Variety, LIII, No. 9 (September 18, 1946).

If his first choice agrees with that of a sufficient
majority, that achievement becomes one of the nominations. However, should his first choice be in the
minority, his vote is applied to his second choice,
or his third, and so on until the voter has helped
to select one of the achievements. In this way, the
entire voting group has a voice in the ultimate selec-
tions. Voters are not obligated to list more choices
than they really have, but if only one choice is expressed, and it is in the minority, the ballot becomes
void, and cannot help in the selection of another
achievement.[120]

Ever since the ninth Annual Awards (1936), Price

Waterhouse & Company, a firm of certified public accoun-

tants, has been assigned the responsibility of counting and

verifying all ballots. Up through the twelfth Annual

Awards (1939), the names of all winners were released to

the press prior to the actual presentation ceremonies.

From that time through the twentieth annual awards (1947),

the names of all winners were kept secret until the actual

presentations.[121]

The first awards given by the Academy were

---

[120]Unpublished papers of the Academy of Motion Picture Arts and Sciences.

[121]The names of all winners were kept secret up
through the twenty-eighth Annual Awards (1955). From the
twenty-ninth Annual Awards (1956) through to the present
(1966) the Honorary, Scientific or Technical, and Thalberg
Memorial Awards have been announced in advance, but the
names of all other winners are kept secret until the moment
of presentation at the annual ceremonies.

authorized by the Board of Directors on July 2, 1928 "to

encourage advancement in the arts and sciences of motion

pictures."[122] Twelve awards were to be given for the fol-

lowing achievements:

> Best performance by an actor
> Best performance by an actress
> Best dramatic directing
> Best comedy directing
> Best cinematography
> Best art directing
> Best engineering effects
> Best original story writing
> Best adaptation
> Best title writing
> Most outstanding production
> Most artistic or unique production[123]

As it turned out the Academy gave two awards for cinematog-

raphy, one to Charles Rosher for _Sunrise_, and the other to

Karl Struss for the same film. They also gave two special

awards, one to Warner Brothers' Studio for producing

The Jazz Singer, as the "pioneer talking picture which

revolutionized the industry," and the other to Charles

Chaplin for "versatility and genius in writing, acting,

directing and producing _The Circus_."[124] In addition the

Academy made twenty honorable mention awards, a practice

---

[122]Unpublished material from the files of the Academy of Motion Picture Arts and Sciences.

[123]_Ibid._   [124]_Ibid._

which was never continued after that first year of awards since omitting honorable mention awards would "enhance the distinction to be gained by the winners."[125]

The second annual awards are significant since they represented a more solid foundation on which the increased number of awards over the years were added. Offered for the year ending July 31, 1929, they were limited to seven categories (see page 98).

The twentieth annual awards in 1947 included twenty-eight categories plus special awards. This increase over the years was a natural reflection of changes in the production of motion pictures. Only four awards for actor, actress, direction, and production were to be unchanged from the first annual awards through to the twentieth in 1947. The four awards for artistic quality of production, comedy direction, engineering effects, and title were never given after the first annual awards in 1927. The awards for supporting actor and actress were first given in 1936 at the ninth annual awards and continued through 1947. The award for art direction was divided into two awards, one for Black & White and the other for Color, in 1940 at the

---

[125]Ibid.

Actor--Best performance or performances, talking or
silent, with special reference to character
portrayal, comedy or dramatic rendition and
speech and diction, if employed.

Actress--Best performance or performances, talking
or silent, with special reference to character
portrayal, comedy or dramatic rendition and
speech and diction,if employed.

Director--Best achievement or achievements in the
art of direction, talking or silent, comedy or
drama, with special reference to character developments, originality of treatment, coordination of sound or audible speech, if employed,
and excellence of craftsmanship in directing as
a whole.

Writer--Best achievement or achievements in writing
for the screen, silent or talking, original or
adaptation, with special reference to construction, originality of treatment, character development, theme, consistency, dialogue, and general
excellence of the whole.

Cinematographer--Best achievement or achievements in
cinematography with special reference to photographic art and quality.

Art Director--Best achievement or achievements in set
designing with special reference to art quality,
correct detail, story application, and originality.

Production--Best motion picture production, silent or
talking, drama, comedy, or musical production,
with special reference to quality, public appeal,
general excellence and all elements that contribute to a motion picture's greatness.[126]

---

[126]Annual Report, Academy of Motion Picture Arts
and Sciences, 1929.

thirteenth annual awards and continued through 1947. The award for assistant direction was first given at the sixth annual awards in 1932-33 and discontinued after the tenth annual awards in 1937. Cinematography was divided into two awards for Color and Black & White in 1939 at the twelfth annual awards and continued through 1947. An award for dance direction was given only for the eighth, ninth, and tenth annual awards in 1935, 1936, and 1937. An award for film editing was given beginning with the seventh annual awards in 1934 and continuing through 1947. Awards related to music scoring demonstrated a recognition of the differences in film types. An award for music scoring was given from the seventh annual awards in 1934 through the tenth annual awards in 1937. This was changed to two awards for best score and original score for the eleventh annual awards in 1938 through the thirteenth annual awards in 1940. This was changed for the fourteenth annual awards in 1941 to two awards for scoring a dramatic picture and scoring a musical picture. These two awards were continued through 1947, except that the scoring of a dramatic picture was changed for the fifteenth annual awards in 1943 to scoring a dramatic or comedy picture. An award for song was first given at the seventh annual awards in 1934 and continued through 1947. Two awards, one for Black & White and the other for Color, were given for interior decoration from the fourteenth annual awards in 1941 through 1947; however the name of interior decoration was changed to set decoration for the twentieth annual awards in 1947. Awards under the general category of short subjects included cartoons, comedy, novelty, color, 1-reel, and 2-reel. The award for cartoons was first given at the fifth annual awards in 1931-32 and continued through 1947. The award for comedy was given only for the fifth annual awards through the eighth annual awards in 1935, and the same was true for the award for novelty. The award for color was given only for the ninth and tenth annual awards in 1936 and 1937. Awards for 1-reel and 2-reel were first given at the ninth annual awards in 1936 and continued through 1947. The first award for sound recording was given at the third annual awards in 1928-1929 and continued through 1947. An award for special effects was first given at the thirteenth annual awards in 1940 and continued through 1947. Awards under the general category of writing included achievement, adaptation, original screenplay, original story, screenplay, and title. The award for achievement was given only twice for the second and third annual awards in 1928-29 and

1929-30. The award for adaptation was given at the first
annual awards in 1927-28, the fourth annual awards through
the seventh annual awards in 1930-31 through 1934, and
finally at the eleventh annual awards in 1938. The original
screenplay award was first given for the thirteenth annual
awards in 1940 and continued through 1947. The original
story award was given from the first annual awards in 1927-
28 through 1947 except for two years on the occasions of
the second and third annual awards in 1928-29 and 1929-30.
The screenplay award was first given at the eighth annual
awards in 1935 and continued through 1947. As mentioned
previously the award for title was only given at the first
annual awards. The documentary awards were for short subject and feature, and were given from the fifteenth annual
awards in 1942 through 1947 except that the feature award
was not given one year at the time of the nineteenth annual
awards in 1946. The scientific or technical awards were
divided into Class I, Class II and Class III. The Class
III award was given every year from the fourth annual
awards in 1930-31 through 1947. The Class II award was
given every year from the fourth annual awards in 1930-31
through 1947 except for the eleventh, twelfth, thirteenth,
eighteenth, and nineteenth annual awards. The Class I

award was given only at the time of the fourth, ninth, tenth and thirteenth annual awards. The Thalberg memorial award, for consistent high quality of production, was given on the tenth, eleventh, twelfth, fourteenth, fifteenth, sixteenth, seventeenth, and nineteenth annual awards. The special awards, for an outstanding achievement during the year not covered by any standard category, were given every year from the first through the twentieth annual awards in 1947 except on the occasions of the second, third, fourth, and sixth annual awards.[127]

Because of the nature of the medium, the Annual Awards have always received wide public attention. This attention, though certainly motivated to some extent by idol worship, has also resulted from a sincere respect for recognized achievement, as evidenced by participation of leaders in society. For example, in 1931 the Vice President of the United States, Charles Curtis, attended the fourth banquet for presentation of Annual Awards to bring personal greetings from President Hoover. Ten years later President Franklin D. Roosevelt made a special nation-wide radio address to the Academy for the Award ceremony.

---

[127]Unpublished material from the files of the Academy of Motion Picture Arts and Sciences.

Every award system has been attacked by someone for some reason. The Academy's system has been no exception, particularly with the high degree of press attention given to various aspects of the motion picture industry. A review of the press and trade publications for the period covered by this study reveals that the Academy Awards have been criticized or speculated about in every possible way that would make a paragraph or a headline. These range from criticisms as to the manner in which the Awards are presented to the validity of the Award presentation itself. Statements have been made that studio pressures were behind certain awards. This is difficult to substantiate in view of the following facts: no single studio has ever controlled a majority block of voters; awards have been given to films involving studios with practically no permanent number of voters under contract; and, voting cannot be controlled when it is accomplished by secret and unsigned ballots from individuals' homes with the results tabulated by an auditing firm. In the final analysis, awards are the reflection of majority judgments of personnel in the motion picture industry in a comparative evaluation of a given year's production efforts. There is evidence that these judgments have had a definite effect on box office receipts. For example, a

news item in <u>Film Daily</u> on March 18, 1947 reported an increase in the receipts for <u>Best Years of Our Lives</u> after
having won the Best Picture award for 1946.

In any event it is apparent that the growth of the
Award of Merit system has exceeded the founders' expecta-
tions who had not included this facet of Academy work in
the original Constitution and By-Laws. Academy Awards have
now developed into a single aspect of Academy endeavor that
focuses world-wide attention on the motion picture industry.

CHAPTER IV

CONTRIBUTIONS OF THE ACADEMY OF MOTION

PICTURE ARTS AND SCIENCES TO EDUCATION

During their preliminary planning sessions, the
thirty-six founders of the Academy recommended formation of
a College Affairs Committee to be headed by Milton Sills as
Chairman, and including Cecil B. de Mille as a member.
These two members of the College Affairs Committee, together with two other Academy founders, Jesse L. Lasky and
Harry M. Warner, participated in a special series of lectures at the Harvard Graduate School of Business Administration in March of 1927 just prior to the founding of the
Academy.

These lectures reinforced the founders' beliefs
that close relationships should be established with educational institutions. Educational institutions were coming
to the same conclusion. It was concrete evidence of the
climate of the times, as outlined earlier in this study,

for members of the motion picture industry to be invited by Dean Donham of Harvard to "present their own story in their own way before its classes."[1] Although the series of lectures were in keeping with the practice of the School of Business Administration at Harvard to go directly to business for case studies, this particular series was uniquely combined with an announcement by the Harvard Fine Arts Department that it was going to start a special film library composed of the best films of each year.

> In the belief that the achievements in motion pictures deserve recognition as part of the cultural development of the country and must be considered in any serious historical and technical study of art, the Department of Fine Arts of Harvard University, in association with the Fogg Museum and the University Library, plans to establish immediately a library and archive of films, selecting annually those films which are deemed worthy of preservation as works of art.[2]

Joseph P. Kennedy stated that "those at the University accepted the motion picture as something more than an inferior kind of drama."[3]

Some three hundred students and a number of

[1] Joseph P. Kennedy (ed.), The Story of the Films (New York: A. W. Shaw Company, 1927), p. i.

[2] Ibid., p. ix.

[3] Ibid., p. 358.

Professors were in regular attendance at the lecture series
to hear Milton Sills express thoughts which he was to use
later as chairman of the College Affairs Committee, and
which underlie the earliest educational contributions of
the Academy.

> "For the survival of the industry it is necessary
> today to draft men of finer intellectual and cultural
> background, of greater energy, of greater business
> power, and of greater poetic creativeness. I think
> this problem is largely one that concerns our univer-
> sities. Personally I look forward to the day when
> in Harvard and elsewhere, schools of motion picture
> technique may be developed, from which we may draw
> our cameramen, our directors, our supervisors, our
> writers, and great many of our actors. That, to
> my mind, would be the solution of one of the gravest
> problems of our industry."[4]

Educational Institutions

As Chairman of the College Affairs Committee of the
Academy, Milton Sills actively pursued his beliefs on this
matter, and on May 24, 1927, just thirteen days after the
Academy's organization banquet, the Committee held its first
meeting. Members of the Committee were Roy Pomeroy, J. A.
Ball, Sidney Olcott, Cecil B. de Mille, Lotta Woods, and
Jane Murfin. The purpose of the first meeting was to confer
with President Rufus B. von KleinSmid of the University of

---

[4]Ibid., pp. 193-194, quoting Milton Sills.

Southern California regarding the possibility of introducing

suitable motion picture courses into the University curric-

ulum. At this meeting the general opinion was developed

that the college courses should be of two kinds. The first

kind of course would be literary and lead mainly to scenar-

io writing. The second kind of course would be strictly

along technical lines. President von KleinSmid was to pre-

sent the Committee with a tentative outline of the proposed

courses. As Milton Sills reported to the members of the

Academy:

> It was recognized by the Committee and by the Presi-
> dent of the University of Southern California that
> cooperative work of this nature will be of inesti-
> mable value both to the motion picture industry
> and the University.[5]

From this first meeting with President von KleinSmid

a chain of circumstances developed that led to the Univer-

sity of Southern California becoming foremost among univer-

sities and colleges in education and training related to

motion picture production.

Many meetings followed between members of the

College Affairs Committee and representatives of the Univer-

sity of Southern California which led to a plan providing

---

[5]Academy Bulletin, No. 1, June 1, 1927.

for placement in the studios of a limited number of persons qualified to discern the relationship of the various branches of motion picture production to the college curriculum. Instructors in motion picture production, who were also to provide direct liaison between the University of Southern California and the Academy, were thus to be developed. The College Affairs Committee and the University of Southern California selected W. M. MacDonald, a speech instructor at the University, and Lester Cowan, a Stanford graduate, for studio placement. W. M. MacDonald was placed at Metro-Goldwyn-Mayer under Harry Rapf, and Lester Cowan at United Artists under M. C. Levee. Disorganization of practically every branch of motion picture production occurred with the sudden advent of talking pictures while this training was under way. In view of the many uncertainties attending this revolutionary development it was deemed advisable to postpone organization of technical courses as part of the University curriculum until conditions were more stable.[6]

In the meantime, at the suggestion of Lester Cowan, the College Affairs Committee and the Academy Board of

_____

[6]Academy Bulletin, No. XVI, November 22, 1928, p. 6.

Directors approved a plan for the preparation of a syllabus
for a cultural course for colleges to be called "Introduction to the Photoplay." The purpose of the course, to be
organized in consultation with college leaders, was to give
students and faculty members an accurate conception of the
photoplay as an art form and as a social institution. The
Committee believed that such a course was the first logical
step in any program of study of the photoplay in colleges
and universities. Arrangements were made for testing the
course in the Liberal Arts College of the University of
Southern California.

The class "Introduction to Photoplay" met once a
week for a two hour period from February 6, 1929 through
May 29, 1929. A preliminary bulletin announcing the class
had been distributed on the campus during the last of
January 1929, and sixty students were originally enrolled.
Eighteen more were allowed to join the class later, some in
an auditor status, thus bringing the class total to seventy-
eight for the first session.

Karl T. Waugh, Dean of the College of Letters, Arts
and Sciences was director of the course and Mr. W. M.
MacDonald, instructor in Speech, was assigned the particular
duty of Instructor for the course. Mr. MacDonald had, by

this time, completed several months of intensive training in various aspects of motion picture production at the Metro-Goldwyn-Mayer Studio. As Instructor for "Introduction to Photoplay" Mr. MacDonald kept the roll, made the reading assignments, conducted the discussions, and prepared and read the examination papers.

The first meeting of the class was held in Bovard Auditorium since it had been planned to make all lectures open to the general public. The class itself would then adjourn to a smaller room for the question and answer session after the lecture. This idea of opening the lectures to the public was discarded at the request of most of the guest lecturers who felt that the purpose of their appearances would be better served if confined to the actual class. The balance of the class meetings were then held away from the public in the physics laboratory room of the New Science Building. One evening was spent at Paramount Studios observing the operation of sound equipment, and at the Academy rooms in the Roosevelt Hotel to see a sound motion picture program.

As often happens with classes which draw heavily on guest lecturers the course as it was actually given differed somewhat from that appearing in the Photoplay

Bulletin issued by the University of Southern California in January. Appendix IV gives the lecture schedule as it actually occurred and was reported to the Academy membership by Dean Waugh after the course was completed. Dean Waugh also indicated that the number of inquiries concerning the course, the number of requests to register for the course, and the success of the first session justified his making "Introduction to Photoplay" a regular part of the curriculum each year.[7]

Mimeographed copies of the lectures given at the University of Southern California were provided as a text to Stanford University and the University of Iowa who had expressed interest in giving "Introduction to the Photoplay" to their students. In July of 1929 Professor Walter R. Miles of Stanford, who had been following the progress of the first course given at the University of Southern California, announced that Stanford would give the course the following year. Professor Paul R. Farnsworth was selected from the Stanford faculty to be the Instructor and he was given tours of the Hollywood studios in preparation

---

[7] Report to the Academy on "Introduction to the Photoplay" by Karl T. Waugh, Dean of the College of Letters, Arts and Sciences, University of Southern California, August 5, 1929.

for giving the course. Professor Walter R. Miles stated:

> We welcome this chance for contact between the Univer-
> sity and the motion picture industry. The University
> in America, I believe, wants to do its part, it wants
> to cooperate in the education program preparing artis-
> tic men and women who make this field their choice,
> the focus of their interest. In the past the motion
> picture industry has walled itself in--has hedged it-
> self in. The University man has been able to learn
> about other industries; some he could know and under-
> stand thoroughly. But he has not been able to know
> the picture industry. Our whole group have been
> thrilled at seeing the visions of possibilities your
> Academy makes open. It is the chain the binds the
> industry and other groups outside the industry.[8]

Stanford's decision to include the course "Introduction to the Photoplay" was largely the decision of Dr. Ray
Lyman Wilbur, scholar of international affairs, and President of Stanford. In a statement to the Academy:

> Dr. Wilbur appreciated the value of motion pictures
> as a force for bringing understanding between nations,
> and saw a great opportunity for the Academy to serve
> not only the art and the industry, but also society
> in general.[9]

President W. W. Campbell of the University of Cali-
fornia at Los Angeles appointed Dr. Kate Gordon to be the
Instructor for the "Introduction to the Photoplay" course.
Dr. Gordon was a prominent psychologist, and authority on

---

[8]Hollywood Magazine, July, 1929.

[9]Academy Bulletin, No. XVI, November 22, 1928,
p. 5.

aesthetics.

Other colleges and universities, such as Yale, Purdue, Columbia, Mills College, Johns Hopkins, the University of Oregon, and the University of Minnesota contacted the Academy concerning the "Introduction to the Photoplay" course.[10]

Two of the early plans of the College Affairs Committee related to this course were abandoned, probably due to lack of funds, time, and support to carry them to a successful conclusion. The first was to publish the copies of the lectures in a textbook form instead of as mimeograph copies. The second was to record the lectures on Vitaphone or Movietone. Undoubtedly shortages of these newly developed equipments prevented their use at colleges and universities during these early stages; later, each institution had formulated its own course and the project was no longer vital.

In 1928 the Academy sponsored a unique experiment in visual education. The visual education departments of the Los Angeles City Schools, Los Angeles County Schools, San Diego Schools, Pasadena Public School, and California

---

[10]Academy Bulletin, No. XXII, June 3, 1929, p. 10.

Universities had become increasingly convinced that much of

the film in the motion picture studio vaults would be of

value to the schools. Mr. Edward Mayer of the University of

California at Berkeley, on December 19, 1928 requested the

assistance of the Academy members. He discussed the past,

present and future of educational films, and outlined the

role which could be played by strictly entertainment films

in educational situations. He proposed that those films

which had been retired to studio vaults after exhibition to

the public be re-edited and adapted for classroom pur-

poses.[11]

The Committee on College Affairs[12] of the Academy

in 1929 sponsored a project to select, adopt and circulate

a sample film to ascertain if indeed there was a demand

among educational institutions for such a service. The

Committee, after a careful consideration of available films,

finally selected Robin Hood as a pilot film because of the

careful historical research which had gone into its

---

[11]Academy of Motion Picture Arts and Sciences,
Bulletin, No. XVII, December 22, 1928, p. 5.

[12]Milton Sills, Cecil B. de Mille, Irving Thalberg,
John W. Considine, Jr., Beulah Dix Flebbe, Clara Beranger,
Lotta Woods, Edward J. Montagne, Chandler Sprague, Paul
Sloane, J. A. Ball, Roy Pomeroy, and Daryl Zanuck.

production. Douglas Fairbanks, Sr., as producer and owner,

gave the necessary permission for use of any parts of the

film for educational purposes. A special committee[13] of

educators was formed under the Chairmanship of Charles

Roach, Director of the Visual Education Department of the

Los Angeles City Schools, to select those portions of the

film which were usable.

This committee selected some 885 feet of different

scenes from the eight reels of the feature picture. En-

titled In the Days of Chivalry this edited footage repre-

sented the first educational film of its kind to be re-

leased to the schools. Prints in both 16mm and 35mm were

made available to schools throughout the United States, to-

gether with a teaching aid booklet which provided the fol-

lowing for use by teachers receiving the film:

1. Recommendations for use of the film.

2. A summary of film content by scenes.

3. A listing of proposed topics for class dis-

cussion.

---

[13]Members of the committee were Marian Isreal,
Assistant Director of Visual Education, Los Angeles County
Schools; Harry H. Haworth, Supervisor of Visual Education,
Pasadena Public Schools; and Marian Evans, Director of
Visual Education, San Diego City Schools.

4. A listing of problems and activities for
   students.

5. Descriptive details of such items in the film
   as armor and falconry.

6. A listing of subject matter recommended for further research by the student.

7. A recommended bibliography of related books on
   medieval life and times.

8. A partial listing of still photographs made from
   the film together with data on their availability.

The Academy further sponsored the distribution of
the film and training aid booklet on a cost basis only.
The response by schools throughout the country indicated the
value of such use of footage from feature productions.
The overall success of this project by the Academy was to
lay the groundwork among educators and motion picture production personnel for future programs such as the ultimate-
ly organized Teaching Film Custodians group.[14]

The cooperative dealings between the Academy and
the University of Southern California, beginning with the

---

[14]Unpublished papers, Academy of Motion Picture
Arts and Sciences.

first meeting on May 24, 1927 with President von KleinSmid,
eventually led to the founding of a Cinema Department at
the University of Southern California in 1932. The course
"Introduction to the Photoplay" under Dean Waugh of the
College of Letters, Arts, and Sciences was given in 1929
and 1930 with W. M. MacDonald as Instructor. In 1931
MacDonald joined Dr. Morkovin of the Sociology Department
who was also giving some cinema courses. Dr. Morkovin had
begun his work with a series of lectures in 1929 on the
psychological aspects of motion pictures with Academy
assistance in the collection and arrangement of material.[15]

Courses in photography, which included some cinema,
were given by Professor Nye in the Physics Department
during 1929, 1930, and 1931. These courses were discontinued with the formation of the new Cinema Department in
1932 as a result of the work of Dr. Morkovin. In this year
the Cinema Department of the University of Southern California offered the first Bachelor of Arts degree with a major
in Cinema ever given in the United States.[16]

---

[15] Academy Bulletin, No. XXIII, July 9, 1929, p. 6.

[16] In 1936 the Cinema Department of USC offered the
first M.A. in Cinema, and in 1958 the first Ph.D. in
Communications with a major in Cinema.

With these accomplishments at the University of
Southern California the prophecy made by Milton Sills in
1928 was carried out. Milton Sills had stated:

> Without the Academy the individual branches of our
> industry would have found it very difficult to estab-
> lish relations with that other vast education branch
> of our community life, the Universities. The Univer-
> sity is not merely a highbrow institution. It edu-
> cates and sends forth people of every walk of life
> prepared to meet the problems and conditions of their
> particular lines of work. The motion picture has
> never had any college standing or recognition.
> Through this Academy, if our plans now under way
> are successfully carried out, the motion picture
> will be placed on an equality with other arts in
> their cultural and social aspects.[17]

In 1943 the University of California at Los Angeles
requested Academy cooperation in establishing courses in
motion pictures at the University. The University wanted to
organize a permanent department of theatre arts which would
include stage, motion pictures, and radio.

A Joint Committee[18] composed of four Academy members and four faculty members was formed. Over a period of
some three years the Committee was considerably enlarged,

---

[17]Academy Bulletin, No. XVI, November 22, 1928,
p. 3.

[18]Members from the Academy were Charles Coburn, Mary
E. McCall, Jr., E. J. Mannix, and Dore Schary. Members
from the University were Dean J. Harold Williams, Alfred E.
Longenil, Ralph Freud, and Martha Deane.

and all pertinent facets were thoroughly considered. The
final result of the Joint Committee's efforts was the University decision to provide a suitable building for the
Theatre Arts Department and a comprehensive curriculum to
include drama, radio, and motion pictures. The motion picture curriculum was to include such courses as photography,
directing, acting, editing, and music scoring.

An Academy member, Kenneth MacGowan, was invited by
the University to join the new Department with the rank of
full Professor. The Academy agreed to remain in an advisory
capacity as needed.[19]

In addition to these major programs with the University of Southern California and the University of California
at Los Angeles the Academy has been continually active in
support of requests from educational institutions all over
the world. Arrangements were made for interviews with outstanding individuals in the motion picture industry, for
visits to studios and processing laboratories, and for
screenings of particular films. Furnishing information and
material for special programs and studies has been a never-
ending routine matter for the Academy. Bibliographies of

---

[19]Unpublished material from the files of the Academy
of Motion Picture Arts and Sciences.

personnel in the industry, copies of scripts, music scores, special film listings, still photographs of personalities, still photographs of equipment, and references to motion picture publications and special articles in periodicals or trade journals were all part of this.

Schools of music, such as at Dartmouth and the University of Michigan, have made liberal use of the Academy's collection of music scores from motion pictures. Special assistance is given to students working on theses and dissertations. A student at the University of Chicago was assisted in the preparation of his dissertation on the translation of literary classics to motion pictures. Another student at Columbia University received considerable help with his dissertation on Hollywood labor unions.

Naturally the local colleges and universities could best take advantage of the Academy cooperation. It also appears that initial contacts between personnel in the Academy and in the motion picture industry provided the means for continuing liaison so that Academy assistance was no longer required.

The activities of the Academy have been on a world-wide basis from the beginning of its existence. The International Educational Cinematographic Institute of the

League of Nations requested and received Academy cooperation in providing a great deal of information on motion picture practices which was used by the Institute in their efforts to advance motion picture arts in all countries of the world. Educational centers in such areas as France, Sweden, England, Ethiopia, India, Arabia, Argentina, and Canada have been provided with information and material to meet special needs. Prize winning still pictures from the Academy sponsored still photo exhibits have been sent to schools in various parts of the world.

In 1945 the Executive Director of the Academy, Mrs. Margaret Herrick, was appointed to serve on the Academic Board of Stephens College. The significance of this lies in the yearly conference of thirty colleges at Stephens which provides them with a contact to all aspects of the motion picture industry.

There was a tendency for the Academy to record in some detail the early cooperative efforts with educational institutions. Later, as these matters became quite routine, the Academy records only referred to educational cooperation and contributions in the most general fashion. However, those occasional references which have appeared in Academy files have made it possible to select a number of cases of particular interest which are representative of kind rather than quantity.

It must also be emphasized that the Academy has traditionally refrained from continuing in any given specific problem area once a stimulus was provided to existing organizations to carry it on. In this sense the Academy role has been that of an instigator for the benefit of the motion picture industry, passing on to other matters as the area of particular concern was taken care of by other means. This is particularly apparent on the technical side where the photographic industry, with its increased alertness to technological advancements and self-training, no longer regarded the Research Council as an advisory group but rather as an operational, product-orientated group. Similarly, the educational institutions continued to carry out long range programs based on their own achieved capability after initial detailed assistance was provided.

Soon after its formation, the Academy assisted both the University of California at Los Angeles and the University of Sydney, Australia in preparation for a debate on the subject, "Resolved, that the world would be better off without movies." Both teams were provided with background

materials, and given extensive tours of the motion picture
studios. The success and general interest shown in this
cooperative effort led to similar requests from other colleges.[20]

The first of a series of talking picture addresses
planned by the Academy for the use of colleges and other
educational institutions was completed in December of 1928.
The speech was given by Milton Sills, and was recorded on
Vitaphone at Warner Bros. Studio. The film was given its
first public reproduction during the convention of the
National Association of Teachers of Speech in Chicago on
December 27, 1928. The subject of the talk by Milton Sills
was the sound film, and it formed a part of a paper read at
the convention by Dean Ray K. Immel of the University of
Southern California. Warner Bros. Studio and Eastman Kodak
donated material, facilities, and equipment necessary for
this Academy project. Will Hays, President of the Motion
Picture Producers and Distributors of America, Incorporated,
made a theatre available in Chicago at no cost for the
morning session of the Convention at which Dean Immel gave
his talk and presented the Academy film. The film was so

---

[20]Academy Bulletin, No. XVI, November 22, 1928,
p. 7.

well received that the Convention passed a special resolu-

tion of thanks to the Academy which was forwarded by John

P. Ryan, President of the Association. The resolution in-

dicated:

> The National Association of Teachers of Speech in
> convention assembled at Chicago, Illinois, notes
> with deep appreciation the effort of the Academy
> of Motion Picture Arts and Sciences to keep the
> speech standards of talking pictures on a high
> level and pledges its support and cooperation in
> the continuance of these efforts as vital to the
> cultural standards of the country.[21]

Although a series of talking picture addresses had been

planned by the Academy this one by Milton Sills was the

only one completed. Although no specific record provides

the reason it was undoubtedly due to equipment availability

problems at educational institutions as mentioned earlier

in this study.

Motion Picture Industry

Simultaneously with the Academy's efforts for the

benefit of educational institutions, considerable emphasis

was given to assistance to the members of the motion pic-

ture industry. At a meeting of the Technicians' Branch on

November 16, 1927 the new processes of incandescent

---

[21]Academy Bulletin, No. XVIII, January 17, 1929,
p. 5.

lighting for motion picture photography were discussed; the
unreliable arc lights were being superseded by the tungsten,
mazda, incandescent, or soft light. The branch members
generally agreed that, within the coming year, incandescent
lighting would be in universal use throughout the studios,
and that probably not more than six or seven cinematographers out of the three hundred or so in the Hollywood area
were sufficiently familiar with the new method to photograph a picture using this lighting method.

The Technicians' Branch therefore decided to promote a series of demonstrations of incandescent lighting at
selected studios in cooperation with the Producers' Branch.
They agreed to invite all cinematographers belonging to the
Technicians' Branch, members of the American Society of
Cinematographers, and any other interested technicians.
The prime purpose was to sufficiently acquaint all cinematographers with incandescent lighting and panchromatic film
to make the new process practical when the expected perfec-
tion of equipment made its installation general in the
studios.[22] The industry would never have been able to meet
public demands had the cinematographers continued to await

[22]Academy Bulletin, No. 5, November 25, 1927, p. 6.

adequate natural lighting for each day's shooting or to rely
on the cumbersome and noisy arcs with their requirement for
continuous adjustment.

The series of demonstrations conducted fro the benefit of the cinematographers was given during the period from
January 18, 1928 through March, 1928. The Technicians'
Branch had decided to incorporate a series of comparative
tests along with the demonstration. These tests compared
the value of mazda and incandescent illumination to arc
lighting. Each studio operating in Hollywood and vicinity
received two questionnaires, one of January 5 when the
tests were started, and the second on March 22 when the
tests were completed. The purpose of the questionnaires
was to ascertain studio conditions and the results of their
operations with relation to the use of incandescent illumination before and after the demonstrations. Replies to
the first questionnaire revealed that only five studios had
been operating with incandescent illumination, and five others had been running partial experiments and investigations.
The replies to the second questionnaire showed that four
more studios had begun immediate operation with incandescent
light as a direct result of the Academy demonstrations.

There were ten public demonstrations held in the

evenings at Warner Bros. Studio. The average attendance for these sessions was 150 which included cinematographers, electricians, and laboratory technicians. One demonstration was held in the lobby of the Roosevelt Hotel before a group of 500 people, and another was held on the grounds of the Garden Court Apartments on Hollywood Boulevard, which attracted a public gathering of some 2,000 people.

The first two night demonstrations, and the last outdoor demonstration, included comparative shots made with both arc and incandescent illumination. All others were made with incandescent alone, except one when mixed illumination of mazda, arc, and Cooper-Hewitt lights were employed. In addition to the major demonstrations at night there were some 74 individual periods of tests made during the day hours by approximately 40 different cameramen. The total negative footage exposed was 72,604 feet contributed together with the positive by Eastman, DuPont and Agfa companies. The laboratory work was done by various laboratories chosen by the cinematographer responsible for the particular test. The film was cut and edited by a special committee of the American Society of Cinematographers. The edited film was approximately 7,000 feet in length, and was exhibited at a meeting of the Academy and the American

Society of Cinematographers at the Hollywood Chamber of Commerce on the evening of April 17, 1928.

Reel one was a series of titles explaining the purposes of the tests and demonstrations followed by a series of test shots showing the relative intensity of illumination provided by arc and mazda lighting. Reel two showed a comparative test of arc and mazda with relation to colors. Reel three was exclusively night exteriors with green foliage background using arc and mazda. Reel four was a selection of the highest quality reached with mazda lights during the demonstrations without an attempt to compare with arc lighting. Reel five showed the quality of mazda for lighting sets particularly the size of a hotel lobby, and also included close-ups of actors to show effects on make-up. Reel six showed the possibilities of lighting effects with mazda equipment. Reel seven was devoted to tests of color charts. Reel eight showed the mechanical defects of mazda at the present stage of development. The most noticeable defects were rings and streaks caused by elements in the spot equipment. Reel nine showed the mixed use of different lights including mazda, arc, Cooper-Hewitt and neon tubes.

As a result of these demonstrations cinematographers

and other members of the motion picture industry became
better acquainted with what was then a new form of illumination. The value and limitations of incandescent lighting
were shown. Lamps, carbons and equipment for both mazda
and arc illumination were improved, and the make-up of actors was corrected.[23] The success of this series of demonstrations for the benefit of the motion picture industry was
generally agreed upon, and in addition to the results of
the questionnaire many leaders in the industry made special
comment to the Academy. For example, Mr. R. E. Houck of
Metro-Goldwyn-Mayer said:

> There is no question in our mind that these tests
> have been very productive. They are responsible,
> in a great degree, for the interest generally shown
> by both technicians and manufacturers and will be
> responsible for future results. From a point of
> education they have been wonderful.[24]

Mr. D. L. Faralla, the Business Manager of First National
Studios, commented:

> In regard to value, the tests have been instructive
> and educational to cameramen, electricians and labo-
> ratory men. As to results, they have proven that
> certain shots can be made with incandescents which

---

[23]Report of Annual Meeting, Academy of Motion Picture Arts and Sciences, November 3, 1928, p. 2.

[24]Academy Bulletin, No. 5, November 25, 1927, p. 6.

were thought impossible. I believe they will save
the producer a lot of money on locations, as well as
in the studio.[25]

At the same time as the course "Introduction to
Photoplay" was being organized in 1928 for college use, a
different type of course was being set up for studio employees. The College Affairs Committee recommended that the
Technicians' Branch of the Academy cooperate with the University of Southern California in offering through the University Extension Division two courses of lectures for the
benefit of Academy members and studio employees in general.
The first course was to "give an understanding of the in-
struments and physical laws involved in the recording and
reproduction of sound and voice for talking pictures."[26]
The College Affairs Committee proposed that Professor Nye,
Head of the Physics Department of the University of Southern California, handle the course with the assistance of
qualified members of the Technicians' Branch. The second
course was to be called "Introduction to Cinematography,"
and its purpose was "to give an appreciation and general

---

[25]Ibid.

[26]Memo to the Executive Committee of the Technicians' Branch from Milton Sills, Chairman of the Academy
College Affairs Committee, dated November, 1928.

understanding of the art of cinematography to persons in the studios who are interested. "[27]

Mr. Joseph Dubray, Secretary of the American Society of Cinematographers and a member of the Technicians' Branch, was recommended as the Instructor for the second course. Mr. Dubray held many conferences with Dean Waugh of the University of Southern California, and it was determined that the course should not be designed to train cinematographers but only to give an appreciation and elementary understanding of the field. This course on cinematography was deemed of less vital importance than the course on sound, and it never actually materialized in the press of other matters.[28]

Unlike the course on cinematography the course on sound did come into being, and it proved to be most successful. This was no doubt due to the importance to the students of knowing something of the new craft of sound recording which was having such an effect on all of motion picture production. The need for a course on sound was expressed by such leaders in the industry as Mr. B. P. Schulberg, who

[27]Ibid.

[28]Supplement dated August 6, 1929 to the Academy Bulletin No. XXIV, August, 1929.

stated:

> When the talking picture revolutionized the industry
> the studios accomplished wonders in adapting them-
> selves to the emergency, but now the time has come
> to take inventory and by educating the studio person-
> nel to lay a strong foundation for future progress.
> Sound is going to be our business for a long time.
> We are not going back to the silent screen ever ex-
> cept for occasional pictures. The need for all motion
> picture creative workers to become intelligently
> familiar with their new tools is a matter of dollars
> and cents and vital to the constant improvement of
> talking pictures which the public demands.[29]

The subject matter of the course was advertised as:

> Part I. A review of necessary preliminaries: the
> nature of sound; the physical characteristics of
> music and speech; the human voice; analysis of the
> sense of hearing. Part II. Electrical recording
> and reproduction of sound, first in a general way
> and then as applied in the production of talking
> motion pictures. Especial attention will be given
> to the instruments and equipment now employed in
> the studios. Problems in acoustics and the artistic
> possibilities of acoustic control will be important
> elements in Part II. Part III. The practical appli-
> cation of physical laws, principles, and theories
> presented in Parts I and II through study and anal-
> ysis of actual problems experienced in talking pic-
> ture production. Studio experts will guide the dis-
> cussion of these problems.[30]

Applications for the sound course were solicited
in August of 1929 for the course to begin on September 17,
1929. Approximately 100 were to be chosen from the applicants who could be from any motion picture studio

---

[29]Supplement dated August 6, 1929 to the Academy
Bulletin, No. XXIV, August, 1929.

[30]Ibid.

department. Applicants needed only to be recommended by an Academy member and pay a $10 tuition fee. The course was planned for a series of ten two-hour lectures over a ten week period. Arrangements had been made with studios to release employees during class hours as necessary. In addition to the lectures, outside reading was required, and examinations were given at the end of the course. No college credit was given for the course, but all persons successfully completing it were given a special certificate.[31]

More than 1,000 applications were received for the course, but the first class was limited to 250 students divided into two sections of 125 each. Dr. A. W. Nye was in charge of the first section, and Professor Vern Knudsen of the University of California at Los Angeles was placed in charge of the second section. The first section met on Tuesday nights and the second section on Thursday nights so that both groups could receive the same guest lectures. All students received an abstract of lectures for their permanent retention.[32] These lectures, revised and updated, subsequently appeared in the Academy published

---

[31] Ibid.

[32] Academy Bulletin, No. XXV, September 25, 1929, p. 2.

book entitled Recording Sound for Motion Pictures, as reported in Chapter III, pages 67-69 of this study.

This sound course was continued at intervals until
all interested studio employees had an opportunity to enroll. By the end of the session on May 22, 1930 over nine
hundred employees from seventeen different studios had
taken the course. Many others, unable to enroll because
they were out of town, received copies of the lectures as
printed in the Academy Technical Digest.[33]

Acknowledgement of the success of the sound course
was expressed by such leaders of the motion picture industry as Irving Thalberg who stated:

> We feel that we cannot emphasize too greatly how
> much this project has advanced the general welfare
> of the industry. It has sold the whole industry
> on the vital principle of cooperative industrial
> education. It has given the personnel an unparal-
> leled opportunity, which they have seized to the
> utmost, to do both themselves and the industry a
> service, not only for today but for the years to
> come. They have received a technical training not
> confined to the methods of their own studios, nor
> to a few narrow principles of application, but em-
> bracing the entire known technique of sound pictures
> from scientific fundamentals to all methods of re-
> cording and reproduction. The lectures were held
> from studio to studio, each section of the class
> being carefully drawn from the men and women of all
> studios, ranks and departments; and this has served

---

[33] Annual Report, Academy of Motion Picture Arts and
Sciences, 1930, p. 21.

to develop in all of them a realization of common
interests, and a wide-spread comradeship. The technical leaders of the industry, too, have been drawn
together, by cooperation in administering the course.
The monetary value of all these services of the School
in contributing to industrial education, cooperation,
and morale, is beyond computation.[34]

In 1936 the Research Council of the Academy decided
that attention should be again directed to providing
courses of study for the benefit of personnel in the motion
picture industry. A Committee on Industrial Education under the Chairmanship of Dr. J. G. Frayne was established,
and was composed of Barton Kreuzer, Dr. Burton F. Miller,
William Thayer, and Ralph Townsend of the Academy. The
Committee was assigned the task of investigating the current needs for vocational education among motion picture
studio employees, and establishing such courses as deemed
necessary. After a survey, the Committee decided that the
most critical area was in the sound field because of the
large number of technical advancements which had been made
since the courses given in 1929 and 1930. Plans were developed for a course in the fundamentals in sound recording,
and announcements were sent to the studios.

---

[34]Irving Thalberg, "Technical Activities of the
Academy of Motion Picture Arts and Sciences," Journal of
the Society of Motion Picture Engineers, XV, No. 1 (July,
1930), 3-16.

Some 206 applications were received from which the Committee, together with the heads of studio sound departments, selected 100 persons. This number was divided into two classes of 50 each which met twice a week in the fall of 1936 under the instruction of Mr. A. P. Hill of Electrical Research Products, Incorporated. In consideration of the number of applications it was decided to repeat the course in the spring of the following year for an additional group of 50 sound technicians. Concurrently with this second session on the fundamentals of sound recording an advanced course was given for a select group of 50 out of the 100 who had completed the fundamental course. The advanced course was conducted by Fred Albin, L. E. Clark, John Hilliard, and Harry Kimball of the Academy.

Lectures from both the advanced course and the course on fundamentals were revised with additional data and published in book form as reported in Chapter III, pages 70-71 of this study. The book was published in 1938 under the title Motion Picture Sound Engineering.

In addition to these major programs, the Academy served to advance the professional and technical education of its members in a variety of ways. The facilities of the Academy were gradually improved over the years to

provide all members with the benefits of a complete library
on motion pictures and quality film projection equipment.
Individual branches, at their scheduled meetings, conducted
a program of reports on topics of current interest to their
members. A brief review of some of the early presentations
provides a type of commentary on motion picture development
from a historical point of view, and are well worth considering in this study.

In 1928, the College Affairs Committee, to stimulate
presentations of value to Academy members, arranged for
faculty members from various educational institutions to
make surveys of the technical activities of interest to
them in the motion picture industry. Milton Sills, Chairman of the Committee, reported to the Academy:

> As the relation of their academic knowledge to our
> problems becomes clear, and as they see opportunities
> to make contributions to the solution of these prob-
> lems, they are invited to submit papers to be read
> at Academy sessions.[35]

This action resulted in such reports as that given by Dr.
Vern O. Knudsen, Associate Professor of Physics at the
University of California at Los Angeles, who presented a
talk entitled "Acoustics Applied to the Recording and

---

[35]Academy Bulletin, No. XIV, September 18, 1928,
p. 3.

Reproduction of Sound" which contained special references to
the studio sound proof stages. Dr. Feree and Dr. Rand, of
Johns Hopkins University, who were leading authorities in
physiological optics, made a survey with a view to making
some contribution to the solution of the problem.of securing
stereoscopic effects on the screen.[36] Considering the complexity of their undertaking as compared with the technology
of the time, it is not surprising that they did not immediately resolve the problem.

Three presentations selected from those given in
1928 through 1930 provide an interesting review of the consideration being given to problems raised by the sound film.

Helen Miller Senn, from the Department of Speech,
Portland Center, University of Oregon, talked about the importance of voice in sound films. She said in part:

The average stage voice of today is not of the high
standard that the Vitaphone or Movietone of the
future will demand. We shall need far better voices.
There must be special training for the microphone.
There need be no straining of the voice that it may
carry to the farthest parts of the theatre. The
microphone will be so perfected that it will reproduce minutely every shade and variation of voice
of the character from the slums or the character from
the elite of society. Voice without pantomime cannot

[36]Academy Bulletin, No. XVI, November 22, 1928,
p. 7.

show the same depth of emotion that it can with
pantomime.[37]

Carey Wilson, screen writer, spoke to what would finally be an accepted practice when films no longer used
sound for sound's sake:

> I am in favor of eliminating any sound effects which
> are so incidental to our everyday life that we would
> pay no attention to them if it weren't for the sheer
> novelty of realizing that we can hear them rattle, or
> whistle, or stutter, or gurgle. We go through life
> constantly unconscious of sounds to which we are ei-
> ther accustomed or which have no significance to us
> at the moment. So far, the screen has been magnify-
> ing the importance of such sounds for the purpose of
> impressing the audience it is listening to a sound
> picture.[38]

The third talk by Robert Edeson, Chairman of the
Executive Committee of the Actors' Branch, was in reaction
to studios bringing actors to Hollywood from the legitimate
stage to appear in early sound films. He stated in part:

> Audible film problems face not only the players from
> silent pictures--they confront stage actors as well.
> Talking into microphones, you see, is much different
> from standing on the stage and filling an auditorium
> with the sound of one's voice. In the instances of
> the first talking pictures, the novelty of hearing the
> human voice from the screen was sufficient to carry
> popular interest. With this experimental period

---

[37]Academy Bulletin, No. XIV, September 18, 1928,
p. 3.

[38]Supplement dated August 6, 1929 to the Academy
Bulletin, No. XXIV, August, 1929, p. 3.

passed, we face the task of perfecting the speaking
voices of all those who address the microphone.[39]

One of the most interesting and farsighted presentations to Academy members was given by W. B. Pettus, Head of
the North China Language School in Peking, China, who discussed the potential importance of the talking picture in
promoting international understanding and good-will by increasing the knowledge of different languages. He pointed
out that Hollywood could become one of the greatest factors
in the promotion of a knowledge of English. Mr. Pettus emphasized:

> When men can freely communicate with each other in a
> mutually understandable world language there will be
> less friction, misunderstanding and war. English is
> rapidly becoming the world language.[40]

He also touched upon what he felt was a serious obligation
of the motion picture industry when he stated:

> It may not be out of place to point out a serious
> weakness in American life which is reflected on the
> screen and depicted on the stage and which has had
> an adverse effect upon the development of American
> influence in other countries. We are a people who
> are very rich in opprobrious epithets which we apply
> to the peoples of other lands. We have insulting
> nicknames for all foreigners, and some of our

---

[39]Academy Bulletin, No. XXIX, February 27, 1930,
p. 6.

[40]Academy Bulletin, No. XIV, September 18, 1928,
p. 5.

playwriters and actors are accustomed to representing
foreign peoples as criminals or fools. There must
be both criminals and clowns, and it is entirely possible to draw them from any country without giving
offense, if the people of that country are also represented among the more desirable characters.[41]

After installation of the new projection and sound
equipment in the Academy offices immediate use was made of
it for the benefit of the members. On March 29, 1929 Electric Research Products, Incorporated, gave a demonstration
for representatives of the sound departments of various
Hollywood studios. The demonstration included a sound educational film made by the Bray Company which showed the action of human vocal organs and the ear.[42]

This was to be the beginning of the Academy's exhibition of exceptional sound and silent films for the interest and instruction of its members. Early emphasis was
placed on those films which showed new methods of treatment
or technical advances. However, members were quick to
point out that few theatres catered exclusively to those
discriminating few to whom an unusual or exceptional motion
picture has a special appeal. They indicated four categories of films which should be sought for:

---

[41]Ibid.

[42]Academy Bulletin, No. XX, April 8, 1929, p. 4.

1. The best of European films.
2. Films produced for special groups such as psychologists and educators.
3. American films which are not profitable commercially, but of special interest.
4. Experimental films which use new inventions or unusual subjects such as microscopic studies.[43]

The Academy made contact with the Amateur Cinema League, Incorporated, of New York City as a potential source of unusual films which would be of interest in keeping with the desires of its members.

One such film screened with the cooperation of the Amateur Cinema League, Incorporated, was a single reel of silent film entitled The Fall of the House of Usher. It had been made by Dr. J. S. Watson, Jr., and Melville Webber of Rochester, N. Y., and received favorable professional comment from Academy members.[44]

Another film, also screened with the cooperation of the Amateur Cinema League, had been made in Siam by B. Juangbhanich who was in America on a scholarship from Bangkok, Siam. The film was silent, eight reels in length, and starred Juangbhanich and his wife. He explained that as the photographer he had placed the camera in position for a

---

[43]Academy Bulletin, No. XXIII, July 9, 1929, p. 5.

[44]Academy Bulletin, No. XXV, September 25, 1929, p. 5.

small boy to operate while he played the leading role. The
entire cast was amateur. Juangbhanich further explained
that books from the United States provided the information
necessary to produce the film.[45]

The Academy provided these programs of special film
showings at irregular intervals during the period covered
by this study, and have done so ever since. There has been
no particular system under which the films have been selected and shown. In many instances the office staff have
heard of a particular film which they know the members
would be interested in, and have arranged for screening it
with the approval of the Board of Governors.

The programs of film classics and unusual films
shown during 1941 provide a good example of the types of
films shown in later years. Through the courtesy of the
Museum of Modern Art in New York the Academy obtained such
films as Intolerance, Greed, Potemkin, Grandma's Boy, and
What Price Glory. From other sources the Academy obtained
the War Reporting Films of Canada, Ni Sangre Ni Arena from
Mexico, British wartime short films, documentary works of
Joris Ivens, and Boy Saint Gyandev, the first talking

---

[45]Academy Bulletin, No. XXVI, November 1, 1930,
p. 6.

feature to reach the United States from India.[46]

Military

In 1930 the Academy made its first contributions to
the training of the military in the field of motion picture
production. In August of that year Lieutenant Colonel W. E.
Prosser of the Signal Corps made arrangements on behalf of
Major General George S. Gibbs, Chief of the U. S. Signal
Corps, U. S. Army, for the training of officers who were to
organize and administer the production of motion pictures
in the Army. The Academy Technical Bureau was assigned the
task of working out a specific course of instruction which
would include both observation and actual experience at
various studios in all facets of motion picture production
over a nine months' period. The first officer selected for
this training was Captain F. W. Hoorn who arrived in October to begin his period of instruction.[47] The Research
Council of the Academy reported in 1941 that one officer
from the Army Signal Corps had been trained each year for
an eight year period. These officers were given personal

---

[46]Annual Report, Academy of Motion Picture Arts and
Sciences, 1941, p. 2.

[47]Academy Bulletin, No. XXXVI, November 1, 1930,
p. 5.

coaching by studio technicians, and operated some equipment under close supervision. This provided them with an important background of information which they could later apply in Army production.[48]

Douglas W. Gallez, in a presentation to the Society of Motion Picture and Television Engineers in 1963 on the training of Army personnel for motion pictures and television emphasized the importance of this training under the Academy by stating:

> Moreover, the Signal School lacked the capability
> of instruction in the use of equipment, and the War
> Department had no more than $200 available to pay
> for officer tuition in film techniques. The situa-
> tion changed in 1930. The Research Council of the
> Academy of Motion Picture Arts and Sciences agreed to
> sponsor a limited number of Signal Corps officers for
> annual photographic training in Hollywood. Thus was
> laid the foundation upon which was built the immense
> pictorial accomplishments of the past twenty years.[49]

It was largely because of this connection with the Army that Darryl F. Zanuck, Chairman of the Research Council of the Academy, volunteered the cooperation of the Research Council in the production of Army training films at

---

[48]Gordon S. Mitchell, Personal correspondence, January 19, 1966.

[49]Douglas W. Gallez, "Training Army Personnel for Motion Pictures and Television," Journal of the Society of Motion Picture and Television Engineers, LXXII (April, 1963), 281-283.

the beginning of World War II.[50] The numbers of personnel

in the armed forces had increased together with the need

for training films in a quantity beyond the production capa-

bility of the Signal Corps motion picture production units.

The Academy Research Council arranged for studios

to undertake the production of Army training films entirely

on a non-profit basis. No charges were made for studio

overhead, equipment, stage space, studio property, or other

facilities used in the production of training films. Many

individuals contributed their time and talent at no cost to

the government. The only actual costs to the government

were for film stock, processing, and some labor. The films

were all produced under the supervision of Signal Corps

officers stationed with the Academy Research Council in a

liaison capacity. In addition the Army assigned a Techni-

cal Advisor to each film project to ensure the correctness

and accuracy of the film. Some of the kinds of Army train-

ing films produced were: Sex Hygiene, The 60MM Mortar,

The Articles of War, Safeguarding Military Information,

Cryptographic Security, The 37MM Antiaircraft Gun Battery,

---

[50]Mitchell, loc. cit.

Combat Counter-Intelligence, and The AA MG Battery.[51]

By May 1, 1943 over 324 reels of training films had been delivered to the Army. In addition to this training film production the Research Council formed a special committee[52] to establish motion picture and still photography training for personnel of the Army Signal Corps. The training program was started in 1942, and 187 men had completed the motion picture training together with 212 men completing the still photo training by 1943. This program was carried out at no cost to the government. Over 59 volunteers[53] from the motion picture industry participated in this training as instructors.[54]

Thus by 1947 the Academy had a record of contributions to education which varied from major programs to

---

[51]Annual Report, Academy of Motion Picture Arts and Sciences, 1941, pp. 5-6.

[52]The committee members were Gordon S. Mitchell, Nathan Levinson, and John Aalberg.

[53]The volunteers included such individuals as: William Eglonton, Head of the Camera Department at RKO; John Arnold, Head of the Camera Department at MGM; and Virgil Miller, Head of the Camera Department at Paramount.

[54]Academy of Motion Picture Arts and Sciences, "A Report--The Academy in Wartime," May 1, 1943. An unpublished pamphlet from Academy files.

relatively smaller, but no less important, activities. This
was a direct result of the Academy's understanding of the
importance of establishing relationships with educational
institutions, and of providing educational benefits to members of the motion picture industry. The University of
Southern California and the University of California at Los
Angeles had both benefited by connections with the Academy.
The U. S. Army received training and assistance which,
according to its own records, was responsible for the success of the Signal Corps motion picture program. Training
in the field of sound had been sponsored by the Academy for
members of the motion picture industry at a time when it
was critical to the survival of the industry. Self-improvement and training was provided to Academy members through
various branch activities.

CHAPTER V

CONTRIBUTIONS OF THE ACADEMY TO THE
MOTION PICTURE INDUSTRY

The contributions of the Academy of Motion Picture
Arts and Sciences to the motion picture industry, aside
from that related to education as outlined in the preceding
chapter, covered such areas as the cultivation of public
good-will as well as direct assistance to industry; stimu-
lation toward better pictures and public relations through
annual awards for achievement; technical advances; improvement of labor-management conditions at a critical time in
motion picture history just before the development of more
appropriate organizations created for that specific purpose; and direct and indirect assistance to the government
during World War II.

Membership Support

One of the most valuable contributions of the
Academy to the motion picture industry was in serving as a

forum for the various production personnel. Before the
Academy was founded there had been little attempt to organize groups among the people of the motion picture industry
to exchange creative ideas. Gathering such a wide diver-
sity of talented people to discuss mutual problems was a
significant contribution of the Academy organization. Individual Branches held their own meetings to consider those
matters of special interest to their craft; however, when
the occasion was appropriate, joint meetings were arranged
for the discussion of mutual problems. For example, the
Producers' Branch and the Technicians' Branch frequently
met to hear reports of the progress and development of
technical matters in the studios.

The facilities of the Academy, as outlined in Chapter III of this study, were gradually improved over the
years so that all members had the benefits of the library
and projection facilities to enhance their meetings. A
brief review of some of the early presentations is important in providing a type of commentary on motion picture
history.

At a meeting on August 8, 1929 J. P. Maxfield of
Electrical Research Products, Incorporated, was invited to
talk about acoustical control. He pointed out that

developments in set construction were bringing greater
freedom of movement and expression to the actor, and thus
permitted the director to regain the mobile techniques of
the silent film. This had a corresponding effect on all
writers who could thus prepare scripts utilizing more natural movement of actors. Maxfield said:

> When the right amount of reverberation or echo is
> brought into the set you will find that it makes
> very little difference whether the speaker speaks
> four, ten, or twenty feet away from the microphone.
> The quality changes as it should when the person
> goes away. When a speaker turns his back to the
> microphone and speaks, we get the same effect, the
> same change in the quality of the voice, you would
> expect when a person turns his back to you and
> speaks.[1]

A special sequence of shots from a recently completed film
was then shown to demonstrate the wider latitude afforded
by realization of this principle.[2]

On October 3, 1929 Mr. C. W. Spain of Electrical
Research Products, Incorporated, explained to Academy members the purposes of sound dubbing:

> (1) to even up volume, (2) to make a new master
> record, (3) to take care of defects in an original
> record and (4) to give uniformity of quality to an
> uncut negative. There is also synchronization in

---

[1]Annual Report, Academy of Motion Picture Arts and
Sciences, 1929, p. 30.

[2]Ibid.

adding music or sound effects to a previously recorded sound track or record, the combining of two or
more sound tracks or records and the transferring of
a film record to disc record or vice versa.[3]

Examples of dubbing were shown in a special reel of film

made by Paramount and United Artists. The film included:

An interesting bit was from a James Cruze picture
in which the musical scoring had been recorded first
and the action and dialogue later. Another example
was a scene from "Lummox" with the dialogue in English
and the same scene repeated with the dialogue in German, a remarkable instance of speech substitution, by
accurate cutting and dubbing.[4]

Public Good-will

The good-will engendered by the Academy on behalf

of the motion picture industry over the years covered many

areas of endeavor and began with the Academy itself. It is

appropriate to present some of the examples in more detail

as being of particular interest from a historical stand-

point.

Just prior to the official charter date of the

Academy the founders, acting as the Academy Board of Direc-

tors, sponsored the collection of a contribution by the

motion picture industry for the Mississippi River Relief

Fund. This first effort of the Academy in creating

[3]Ibid., pp. 30-31.   [4]Ibid., p. 31.

good-will for the industry resulted in the presentation of a check for $35,000 to the Mississippi River Relief Fund officials on May 12, just one day after the organization dinner of the Academy on May 11. It is significant that this contribution was in addition to direct donations by the individual studios, members of industry, and a Hollywood Benefit Bowl performance. The Academy collection was more than 10 percent of the total contribution of the Los Angeles area.[5]

In 1929 the Secretary of the Interior, Dr. Ray Lyman Wilbur, who was also the President of Stanford University, requested the Academy assistance and participation in a two day Stanford-Muybridge memorial ceremony on May 7 and 8 to celebrate the fiftieth anniversary of the photography of objects in motion which had been conducted on the old Stanford farm in 1879. The Academy sent L. B. Mayer, William C. de Mille, Clara Beranger, Alex Francis, L. H. Tolhurst, and Lester Cowan as representatives and participants. Mr. Tolhurst gave a special demonstration on the night of May 7 which showed the development of motion picture photography since the first Maybridge experiments.

---

[5] Academy Bulletin, No. 1, June 1, 1927, p. 2.

His demonstration included samples of motion pictures taken
from the earliest days up until 1929. L. B. Mayer and
William C. de Mille gave talks on motion pictures to the
faculty and student body of Stanford University. A reel of
talking pictures had been made of the Secretary of the Interior in Washington, D. C. giving a talk just for the occasion. This reel of film had been made by courtesy of the
Fox Film Corporation, and was shown by means of special
sound and picture equipment provided by Electric Research
Products, Incorporated. The Stanford-Muybridge ceremony
included the unveiling of two tablets, one on the exact spot
where the Stanford-Muybridge-Isaacs experiments were made,
and the other in the memorial court of the University.[6]

That same year President Hoover, as Chairman of the
General Committee for the "Light's Golden Jubilee," requested that the President of the Academy, Douglas Fairbanks Sr.,
serve on the committee which was to honor Thomas Alva
Edison as the creator of electric lighting. The Academy
also participated in a local celebration of this 50th anniversary of Thomas Edison's invention of the incandescent

---

[6]Annual Report, Academy of Motion Picture Arts and
Sciences, 1929, p. 9.

lamp.[7] The Academy, as indicated in Chapter III, pages
77-79 of this study, had elected Edison as its first honorary member in particular recognition of his achievements as
a creator of fundamental inventions in motion pictures and
sound synchronization, and his achievements in lighting.

Also typical of early Academy achievements in good-
will was assistance provided the Reverend J. Edgar Williams
at the request of Stanford University for his lecture on
motion pictures which he gave on tours throughout the
United States. The Academy served as initial contact with
interested individuals in the motion picture industry for
the University Religious Foundation at the University of
California at Los Angeles in its efforts to promote the
establishment and construction of a building devoted to religious activities open to all denominations. The Academy
also made the industry contacts for Mr. W. J. Herwig of the
Narcotic Research Association to help promote a campaign
against the use of narcotics.[8]

The Academy, in the interest of good-will, made its

---

[7]Academy Bulletin, No. XXV, September 25, 1929,
p. 6.

[8]Academy Bulletin, No. XXIII, July 9, 1929, p. 6.

facilities available to numerous organizations and groups
for meetings. In 1928, coincident with the tests and demonstrations on incandescent lighting reported in Chapter
IV, pages 125-130 of this study, the Academy had achieved
cooperative contact with the Society of Motion Picture Engineers. The Academy invited the Society to hold its spring
convention in the Academy rooms from April 9, 1928 through
April 14, 1928. This was the first convention of the
Society of Motion Picture Engineers ever held on the West
Coast. Academy members, many of whom were also members of
the Society, participated in the meetings, and on April 11,
1928 the Academy gave the Society a banquet which was
attended by more than 300 members and guests.[9]

In 1929 the local chapter of the American Projection Society held its meetings in the Academy lounge. This
was particularly advantageous to their group since the
Academy then had facilities for projection of both silent
and talking pictures. This organization consisted of about
ninety of the leading projectionists in the Los Angeles
area, and was primarily interested in the solution of technical problems related to projecting motion pictures. With

---

[9]Report of the Annual Academy Meeting for 1928
dated November 3, 1928, p. 2.

the cooperation of the Academy members matters such as problems of sound reproduction and the care and improvement of
equipment were discussed at these meetings.[10]

In general, the Academy has readily supported any
program of benefit to all connected with the industry. Such
a program was the Motion Picture Relief Fund of America.
The Academy founders created a Benefit Picture Committee
which held its first meeting the same month the Academy
was formed in 1927. The Academy was to sponsor production
of a motion picture the proceeds of which would go to the
Motion Picture Relief Fund of America. The Benefit Picture
Committee arranged for the Writers' Branch to appoint a
special sub-committee the night it met for its own organization on June 8, 1927. The sub-committee was to consider
ideas from all writers for a story to be used in making
the film. By November 25, 1927 preparation of a proposed
story was under way, and the Benefit Picture Committee
could report to Academy membership successful progress.[11]
Unfortunately, support could not be obtained from the
distributing companies, and the benefit film idea was

[10]Academy Bulletin, No. XXIII, July 9, 1929, p. 6.
[11]Academy Bulletin, No. 5, November 25, 1927, p. 4.

abandoned.[12]

The Academy support of the Motion Picture Relief Fund then took the form of urging cooperation of its members in support of the Fund. This became particularly true in 1929 when the Fund was withdrawn from the Community Chest, not as a reflection on that organization, but simply because the Fund was a national organization and its relief had to be extended outside of the Hollywood area. This had the effect of placing the burden for carrying the Fund entirely on the motion picture industry, and the Academy naturally assumed a large share of the responsibility in urging members of industry to support the Fund. As Mary Pickford said in a special address at the 1929 Awards Banquet:

> We, who are so active in the making of motion pictures, and who have prospered more or less are apt to forget, in our rush and hurry and in the excitement of our many interests, those in the many branches of our profession who have been less fortunate either through sickness or old age or other conditions over which they have no control. Many of these have been prominent actors, well known directors, or talented writers, who, for one reason or another, have been left behind in the race. The procession has passed them by, and it is for their aid that the Motion Picture Relief Fund of America was formed.[13]

[12]Annual Report, Academy of Motion Picture Arts and Sciences, 1929, p. 59.

[13]Academy Bulletin, No. XXII, June 3, 1929, p. 4.

Although no further attempts were made by the Academy to undertake projects of the nature of the Benefit Film the record indicates continual support by membership of the programs of the Motion Picture Relief Fund.

On November 7, 1928 the Academy arranged for a special banquet in honor of a group of visiting British journalists who were touring the United States. The Academy records state:

> While delightfully informal in its conduct, it was an effective demonstration of good will in two important ways; first, in its international aspect as a part of our country's welcome to the delegation from abroad with its mission of amity, and second, as a friendly contact of understanding between distinguished leaders of the English language press and responsible representatives of all branches of the motion picture production.[14]

It is well worth noting the substance of talks given at this particular banquet because they point up facets of historical relationships between the motion picture industry of the United States and Great Britain. L. B. Mayer in his talk

> assured the British journalists that motion pictures produced abroad needed only to be good and outstanding productions to command public patronage in this country. There is no such thing as a closed market here. He cited numerous instances, including Quo Vadis,

---

[14] Academy Bulletin, No. 22, 1928, p. 8.

Caberia and Passion. The art of pictures, he said,
like other arts, knows no national or racial limitations.[15]

Sir George Armstrong, of the <u>Daily Chronicle</u> group,

said:

> he and his companions would return to their homes with
> warm and vivid memories of their visit, not the least
> of which would be the exhibitions they had heard of
> talking pictures. They had heard them described as
> talkies or squeakies but they were nevertheless truly
> marvelous.[16]

Harry Warner responded with:

> The squeakies or squawkies are now fixed as the
> established form of motion picture entertainment
> and their part in increasing the world influence of
> the motion picture thereby promoting universal peace
> would be recognized by coming generations.[17]

J. Stuart Blackton, a former Englishman and one of

the pioneers of the development of American silent films,

expressed the opinion that

> English producers had not been forward in keeping
> pace with picture advancement. If an English speak-
> ing union were ever realized, it would be the newly
> perfected talking picture that would be largely
> credited with bringing it about.[18]

Ralph D. Blumenfeld, leader of the British

---

[15] <u>Ibid</u>., pp. 8-9.   [16] <u>Ibid</u>., p. 9.

[17] Academy Bulletin, No. XVI, November 22, 1928,
p. 9.

[18] <u>Ibid</u>.

delegation, spoke on English production:

> In reference to the quota law, companies were being
> organized and shares were being sold on every hand
> in England for the production of motion pictures.
> Nevertheless there would always be a demand for
> American films.[19]

William C. de Mille cautioned the British:

> not to confuse stock-selling with picture production,
> a warning that has been necessary too frequently in
> this country.[20]

But of all the comments made that evening Cecil B.
de Mille had the most hopeful view of the future:

> The motion picture was the one great medium of
> communication for all peoples of the earth and its
> influence was helping to create that spread of knowl-
> edge and understanding that must precede world
> peace.[21]

As indicated in Chapter II of this study the continued acceptance by the public of motion pictures was always of concern to an industry which faced recurring threats
of censorship and boycott practices. Gaining the public
support of nation-wide organizations for films in advance
of their release was considered to be a partial solution
to the problem. Therefore in 1929 the Academy, by arrangement with the Motion Picture Producers and Distributors of
America, set up a series of pre-release screenings at their

---

[19]Ibid.   [20]Ibid.   [21]Ibid.

projection facilities for such organizations as the Ameri-

can Library Association, International Federation of Catho-

lic Alumnae, Federal Council of Churches, American Associa-

tion of University Women, National Congress of Parents and

Teachers, General Federation of Women's Clubs, and the

Daughters of the American Revolution. Five representatives

from each of the organizations were invited to each screen-

ing of new films which were ready for distribution but

which had not yet been publicly exhibited. The representa-

tives made reports on each film to their respective nation-

al headquarters which were then distributed to their vari-

ous branches.[22] The immediate reaction, at least on the

part of the local representatives, was most favorable, as

evidenced by Mrs. Edward Jacobs of the General Federation of

Women's Clubs at the 1929 Anniversary Banquet of the Acad-

emy:

> Every day here at the Academy we are seeing previews
> of the films after they are made. This is a marvel-
> ous opportunity and we are appreciative and we send
> out previews on these films, not only over all the
> United States but into Europe and Canada and even to
> Japan. We are not censors. We boost the best and
> ignore the rest. By advance publicity, as we see
> them long in advance of their bookings, we create an
> interest in these better films. We feel this coopera-
> tion between national clubs and the Academy is going

---

[22] Academy Bulletin, No. XX, April 8, 1929, p. 5.

to result in a great amount of good not only for the public at large but also for the good of the industry.[23]

These screenings were quite properly to become the sole responsibility of the Producers Association which had the prime concern in this area, and was the most appropriate organization to deal with matters related to censorship. In fact, the records show that the Academy was never to assume a major role in the area of concern for censorship of motion pictures. Academy members did give talks to various organizations and civic groups, sometimes arranged through the Academy, but these were primarily individual actions rather than a major Academy effort.

The Academy has not been the official spokesman for the motion picture industry. However as early as 1928 the industry in general recognized that the Academy made an excellent clearing house for information.[24] From that time on the Academy received and handled on a daily basis inquiries from the press, organizations, institutions, and individuals. In 1947, the Academy library kept a record on a day by day basis to determine the workload involved in

---

[23] Academy Bulletin, No. XXII, June 3, 1929, p. 6.

[24] Academy Bulletin, No. XIII, August 11, 1928, p. 2.

this facet of routine business. An average of 300 persons per week, including college students, studio personnel, and members visited the library for assistance. Several thousand telephone calls were received each week asking for specific bits of information on some facet of the motion picture industry or Academy operation.[25]

American silent films had derived considerable revenue from foreign markets over the years through the simple expedient of substituting foreign language titles. The silent picture was inherently an international art form; the sound picture basically nationalistic. A European could see a sub-titled American silent film with no sense of alienism; but no European sub-title could overcome the background of American nasals. The only real solution was to redub the sound tracks, which involved careful revision of dialogue and lip synchronization. In recognition of the major difficulties facing all of the motion picture studios the Academy sponsored a meeting of studio representatives from the foreign departments. As a result of this meeting a committee was formed in 1930 to arrive at simplified and standardized procedure from among the various experiments

---

[25] Academy of Motion Picture Arts and Sciences, Report of the President, May 25, 1948.

that had been tried.[26] The preliminary work of the committee revealed that solution of the basic problem related to
production policies, and casting details. These factors
were more properly under the jurisdiction of the Motion
Picture Producers and Distributors of America than the
Academy of Motion Picture Arts and Sciences. Hence sponsorship of the committee was turned over to the Motion Picture
Producers and Distributors of America. This action on the
part of the Academy was typical in its recognition of common problems, instigating work towards solutions, and turning matters over to a more appropriate organization once
interest and value was proven.[27]

Related to the foreign market for American films
was the importance of stimulating visits by leading representatives of foreign studios. Typical were the contacts
arranged by the Academy between Hollywood studio executives
and technicians and leading representatives of the state-
controlled film industry of Russia. Leon Monosson, Presi-

---

[26]Members of the committee included Paul Kohner,
Geoffrey Shurlock, John Stone, Frank Davis, Jerome Lacken-
bruch, Salvador de Alberich, Leon d'Usseau, Heinz Blanke,
and DeLeon Anthony.

[27]Academy Bulletin, No. XXIX, February 27, 1930,
p. 5.

dent of Amkino Corporation, and Michael Mashonkin, Chief
Engineer of the Central Laboratories of Wire Communication
in Leningrad, were invited in 1930.[28]

The Amkino Corporation was the official representative of the Russian government in all dealings with the
United States concerning motion pictures. Amkino purchased
equipment, distributed Russian films, and handled the release of all American films chosen for showing in Russia.
Monosson was particularly interested in the executive management systems related to film production, and the latest
developments of studio sound equipment. Mashonkin, who had
been surveying motion picture industries throughout the
world, concentrated on all matters related to the acoustic
construction of studios, the transmission problems of sound
recording, and improvements in cameras for sound films.[29]

In November of 1930 the Academy started a practice
which was to be followed over the years by successive staff
members of the Academy. This was to have the Executive
Manager tour various cities to talk to organized groups
representing civic clubs, women's organizations, motion

---

[28]Academy Bulletin, No. XXXVI, November 1, 1930,
p. 5.

[29]Ibid.

picture review groups, leaders of industry, and film boards
of trade. The purpose was to bring the public and the motion picture profession closer together in appreciation and
understanding. It also gave an opportunity to inform the
public of the Academy's programs and achievements. The
Academy Board of Directors saw this as a means to "strengthen the ties between the thinking people of the nation and
those purposes for which the Academy was organized."[30]

In 1941 the Academy sponsored the "First Annual
Hollywood Still Photography Exhibit" for still cameramen in
the motion picture studios. These cameramen worked closely
with their studio publicity personnel who recognized that
special attention for the still cameraman was long overdue.
The idea came from John LeRoy Johnson, Head of Publicity at
Universal, and was readily endorsed by the industry as an
excellent type of institutional publicity. Prints submitted by the studio publicity departments were selected by
various groups of judges including picture editors of the
wire and feature services. The first event attracted considerable attention, and more then 600 prints were entered
and displayed. The collection was sent to New York for a

---

[30] Ibid., p. 7.

month's exhibit at the Museum of Modern Art. It was subsequently divided into six traveling exhibits which went all
over the United States for display in galleries, libraries,
universities, and various photographic organizations. One
of the exhibits was sent to Australia.[31] A second contest
was conducted in 1942, and was equally well received.
Prints from both the 1941 and 1942 contests were sent to
Russia, Australia, and South America.[32] The contest was
discontinued in 1943 due to the wartime shortages of photographic supplies, and not revived until 1946.[33] This contest was given a three-day show in the lobby of the Columbia Broadcasting Studio. Three complete sets of prints
were shipped on tours of the United States. One set was
sent to the Library of Congress, and another to the Museum
of Modern Art in New York.[34]

---

[31]Annual Report, Academy of Motion Picture Arts and
Sciences, 1941, p. 3.

[32]Academy of Motion Picture Arts and Sciences,
"A Report--The Academy in Wartime," May 1, 1943. An unpublished pamphlet from the Academy files.

[33]The 1948 contest toured the British Isles and
South Africa through 1949, and in 1950 the capital cities
of Europe.

[34]Academy of Motion Picture Arts and Sciences,
Report of the President, May 25, 1948.

Awards of Merit

Chapter III, pages 90-104 of this study, explains
the Academy's system for judging the Awards of Merit and
provides a general perspective of the kinds of awards. As
reviewed in Chapters I and II of this study motion pictures
were just beginning to obtain recognition as a possible art
form at the time of the founding of the Academy. The founders of the Academy believed that awards determined by this
organization with ideals and aims would help to dignify the
media of motion pictures. This is particularly true in
consideration of the special awards and the Scientific or
Technical Awards which represent a definite form of contribution to the industry in highlighting and recognizing significant advances of the profession.

The special awards provide a type of historical review of accomplishments in the theatrical film which should
not be overlooked. Warner Brothers Studio received an
award the first year for producing the pioneer talking picture The Jazz Singer which revolutionized the industry.
That same year Charles Chaplin received a special award for
his versatility and genius in writing, acting, directing and
producing the film entitled The Circus. Special awards were
not given on the occasion of the second, third, fourth, and

sixth annual awards. Walt Disney was given a special award
at the fifth annual awards for his creation of the cartoon
character Mickey Mouse. Shirley Temple was given a special
award at the seventh annual awards in 1934 for her contribution to screen entertainment. David Wark Griffith received a special award at the eighth annual awards in 1935
for "his distinguished creative achievements as director
and producer and his invaluable initiative and lasting contributions to the progress of the motion picture arts."[35]
Two special awards were given at the ninth annual awards in
1936. The first went to The March of Time for "its significance to motion pictures and for having revolutionized one
of the most important branches of the industry--the newsreel."[36] The second went to W. Howard Greene and Harold
Rosson for the color cinematography in the Selznick International production entitled The Garden of Allah. In 1937
at the tenth annual awards three special awards were given
by the membership of the Academy. The first went to Mack
Sennett:

For his lasting contribution to the comedy technique

---

[35]Unpublished material from the files of the Academy of Motion Picture Arts and Sciences.

[36]Ibid.

of the screen, the basic principles of which are as
important today as when they were first put into practice, the Academy presents a special Award to that
master of fun, discoverer of stars, sympathetic, kind-
ly, understanding comedy genius--Mack Sennett.[37]

The second special award that year went to Edgar Bergen for

his creation Charlie McCarthy. The third special award was

given to the Museum of Modern Art Film Library for

its significant work in collecting films dating from
1895 to the present and for the first time making
available to the public the means of studying the
historical and aesthetic development of the motion
picture as one of the major arts.[38]

Three special awards were given at the eleventh annual

awards in 1938. The first went to Deanna Durbin and Mickey

Rooney for "their significant contribution in bringing to

the screen the spirit and personification of youth, and as

juvenile players setting a high standard of ability and

achievement."[39] Harry M. Warner received the second award

for his patriotic services in producing a series of histori-

cal short subjects concerning the early American struggle

for liberty. Walt Disney received the third award for his

creation of Snow White and the Seven Dwarfs, which was

"recognized as a significant screen innovation which has

charmed millions and pioneered a great new entertainment

---

[37]Ibid.   [38]Ibid.   [39]Ibid.

field for the motion picture cartoon."[40] Five special awards
were given at the twelfth annual awards in 1939. The first
award went to Douglas Fairbanks Sr. as a commemorative
award, the second to Technicolor Company for bringing three-
color feature production to the screen, the third to the
Motion Picture Relief Fund acknowledging its outstanding
services to the industry, the fourth to Judy Garland for
her outstanding performance as a screen juvenile, and the
fifth went to William Cameron Menzies for the use of color
to enhance dramatic mood in the film Gone with the Wind.
Two special awards were given at the thirteenth annual
awards in 1940. Bob Hope received the first award in recognition of his unselfish services to the motion picture industry. Colonel Nathan Levinson received the second award
for

> his outstanding service to the industry and the
> Army during the past nine years, which has made
> possible the present efficient mobilization of the
> motion picture facilities for the production of
> Army Training Films.[41]

Five special awards were given at the fourteenth annual
awards in 1941. The Canadian National Film Board received
one for distinctive achievement in short subjects

---

[40] Ibid.   [41] Ibid.

Documentary production. Rey Scott received a special

award for

> his extraordinary achievement in producing "Kukan,"
> the film record of China's struggle, including its
> photography with a 16mm camera under the most diffi-
> cult and dangerous conditions.[42]

The British Ministry of Information received a special

award for the documentary production Target for Tonight,

a dramatic presentation of the heroism of the R.A.F. Walt

Disney, William Garity, John N. A. Hawkins, and the RCA

Manufacturing Company received the fourth special award

that year for the advancement of the use of sound in the

motion pictures through production of Fantasia. The fifth

special award went to Leopold Stokowski and his associates

for their creation of a new form of visualized music in

Fantasia, thereby widening the scope of the motion picture

as entertainment and as an art form. Three special awards

were given at the fifteenth annual awards in 1942. The

first went to Charles Boyer for his achievement in estab-

lishing the French Research Foundation as a reference source

for the Hollywood motion picture industry. The second

award was presented to Noel Coward for his outstanding

production achievement entitled In Which We Serve. The

---

[42]Ibid.

third special award was given to Metro-Goldwyn-Mayer Studio
for representing the American way of life in the Andy Hardy
film series. Two special awards were given on the occasion
of the seventeenth annual awards in 1944. The first went
to Margaret O'Brien as the outstanding child actress of
1944, and the second was given to Bob Hope in the form of a
Life Membership in the Academy for his many services to the
Academy. Three special awards were given at the eighteenth
annual awards in 1945. The first went to Walter Wanger for
his six years of service as President of the Academy; the
second to Peggy Ann Garner as the outstanding child actress
of 1945, and the third to the production personnel for The
House I Live In as a tolerance short subject. Four special
awards were given at the nineteenth annual awards in 1946.
The first went to Laurence Olivier for his outstanding
achievement as actor, producer, and director in Henry V.
The second special award was given to Harold Russell for
bringing both hope and courage to his fellow war veterans
through his appearance in the film The Best Years of Our
Lives. The third special award was given to Ernst Lubitsch
for his distinguished contributions to the art of the motion picture. The fourth award was given to Claude Jarman,
Jr., as the outstanding child actor of 1946. The twentieth

annual awards in 1947 brought four special awards. The

first went to <u>Bill and Coo</u> for a novel and entertaining use

of the medium of motion pictures. The second special award

was given to the film entitled <u>Shoe-Shine</u>. This award was

given because the Italian production was considered to be of

superlative quality, made under adverse circumstances. The

third award was presented to Colonel William N. Selig,

Albert E. Smith, George K. Spoor, and Thomas Armat as motion

picture pioneers for their contributions to the development

of the motion picture industry. The fourth special award

was given to James Baskett for his characterization of

"Uncle Remus" in the motion picture entitled <u>Song of the</u>

<u>South</u>.[43]

    It should be noted that the special awards were

given for achievements which were not considered to be

strictly within the categories of other awards. They were

granted by the Board of Directors (Board of Governors) of

the Academy for superlative and distinguished service in the

making of motion pictures, or for outstanding service to the

Academy. They could be given in connection with foreign as

well as domestic productions, and although listed for

---

[43]<u>Ibid</u>.

convenience by annual award years are not limited to that
particular year. They may be in such form as the Board
decides. For example, the Board presented Statuettes
(Oscars), Life Memberships, or Certificates.

The Irving G. Thalberg Memorial Award was established at the time of the tenth annual awards in 1937,
and is given for consistent high quality of production.
The achievement records of individuals responsible for
motion picture production are reviewed by the Board of
Governors, and verbal nominations are made from the meeting
floor. Secret written ballots are taken after the nominations are complete. As many as three ballots are taken to
determine a majority vote of the Board. If a majority vote
is not achieved on three ballots no award is given for that
year. This occurred at the time of the thirteenth, eighteenth, and twentieth annual awards. The Academy rules
stipulate that no individual is eligible to receive the
Thalberg award more than once every three years. The first
Thalberg award at the tenth annual awards in 1937 was given
to Darryl F. Zanuck; the second at the eleventh annual
awards in 1938 to Hal B. Wallis; the third at the twelfth
annual awards in 1939 to David O. Selznick; and the fourth
at the fourteenth annual awards in 1941 to Walter E.

Disney. Sidney Franklin received the fifth Thalberg award
at the fifteenth annual awards in 1942. The sixth Thalberg
award went to Hal B. Wallis, which was his second award, at
the sixteenth annual awards in 1943. The seventh award went
to Darryl F. Zanuck, which was his second Thalberg award,
at the seventeenth annual awards in 1944. Samuel Goldwyn
received the eighth Thalberg award at the nineteenth annual
awards in 1946.[44]

The Scientific or Technical Awards are broken into
Class I, Class II, and Class III. Class I winners receive
an Oscar as the trophy. Class II winners receive a plaque,
and Class III winners are given a certificate of honorable
mention. The Class I award is given for basic achievements
which have a definite influence upon the advancement of the
industry. Class II awards are given for those achievements
which exhibit a high level of engineering or technical merit
and which are important contributions to the progress of
the industry. Class III awards are given for those accomplishments which are valuable contributions to the progress
of the industry.[45]

Only five Class I awards were given from the

---

[44]Ibid.   [45]Ibid.

beginning of Scientific or Technical Awards at the fourth
annual awards in 1930-31 through the twentieth annual awards
in 1947. The first Class I award went, at the fourth annual
awards, to Electrical Research Products, Incorporated, RCA
Photophone, Incorporated, and RKO Radio Pictures, Incorporated, for noise reduction recording equipment. The
second Class I award was presented that same year to DuPont
and Eastman Kodak for the supersensitive panchromatic film.
The third Class I award was presented at the ninth annual
awards in 1936 to Douglas Shearer and the Metro-Goldwyn-
Mayer Sound Department for development of a practical two-
way horn system and a biased Class A push-pull recording
system. The fourth Class I award was presented at the
tenth annual awards in 1937 to Agfa Ansco for the Agfa
Supreme and Agfa Ultra Speed pan motion picture negatives.
The fifth Class I award was given at the thirteenth annual
awards in 1940 to the 20th Century-Fox Film Corporation for
the design and construction of the 20th Century Silenced
Camera developed by Daniel Clark, Grover Laube, Charles
Miller, and Robert W. Stevens.[46]

Twenty-one Class II awards were given from the

---

[46]Ibid.

fourth annual awards in 1930-31 through the twentieth
annual awards in 1947. The first award was given to Fox
Film for their effective use of Synchro-Projection composite
photography; the second to Technicolor for its color cartoon
process; and the third to Electrical Research Products,
Incorporated, for the wide range recording and reproducing
system. RCA Victor Company, Incorporated, was given the
fourth award for their high fidelity recording and reproduction system. The fifth award went to Electrical
Research Products, Incorporated, for development of the
vertical cut disc method of recording sound for motion pictures. The sixth award was to Agfa Ansco for development
of the Agfa infra-red film. E. C. Wente and the Bell Telephone Laboratories received the seventh award for the mul-
ti-cellular high-frequency horn and receiver. The eighth
award went to RCA for the rotary stabilizer sound head.
The ninth award was given to Walt Disney Productions for
the design and application to production of their multi-
plane camera. Eastman Kodak received the tenth award for
developing two fine-grain duplicating stocks. Farciot
Edouart and Paramount were given the eleventh award for
development of the Paramount dual screen transparency camera setup. Douglas Shearer and Metro-Goldwyn-Mayer Sound

Department were given the twelfth award for a method of
varying the scanning width of variable density sound tracks
(squeeze tracks) for the purpose of obtaining an increased
amount of noise reduction. The thirteenth Class II award
was given to the Electrical Research Products Division of
Western Electric Company, Incorporated, for development of
a precision integrating sphere densitometer. RCA received
the fourteenth award for design and development of the MI-
3043 uni-directional microphone. Carroll Clark, F. Thomas
Thompson, and the RKO Radio Studio Art and Miniature Departments were given the fifteenth award for design and construction of a moving cloud and horizon machine. The sixteenth award went to Daniel B. Clark and the 20th Century-
Fox Corporation for development of a lens calibration system and the application of the system to exposure control
in cinematography. Photo Products Department of DuPont received the seventeenth award for development of a fine
grain motion picture film. The eighteenth award went to
Farciot Edouart, Earle Morgan, Barton Thompson, and the
Paramount Engineering and Transparency Departments for
development and practical application to motion picture
production of a method of stereopticon projection of natural color photographs. The nineteenth Class II award was

presented to Stephen Dunn, RKO Radio Sound Department, and RCA for additional development of the electronic compressor-limiter. C. C. Davis and the Electrical Research Products Division of Western Electric were given the twentieth Class II award for development and application of an improved film drive filter mechanism. The twenty-first Class II award went to C. R. Daily and the Paramount Film Laboratory for the development and first practical application to motion picture and still photography of a method of increasing film speed as first suggested to the industry by the E. I. DuPont de Nemours & Company.[47]

The Class III awards were given for those accomplishments which the Academy considered to be valuable contributions to the progress of the industry. A total of seventy-seven Class III awards were given from the time of the fourth annual awards in 1930-31 and the twentieth annual awards in 1947. The following twelve Class III awards are examples which are representative of the kind of accomplishements honored by the Academy. The first award was given to Electrical Research Products, Incorporated, for the moving coil microphone transmitters, and the second

[47]Ibid.

to RKO Radio Pictures, Incorporated, for the reflex type microphone concentrators. RCA Photophone, Incorporated, received the third award for ribbon microphone transmitters. The fourth award was given to Eastman Kodak for its Type II-B sensitometer. Bell and Howell Company received the seventh award for their development of the Bell and Howell fully automatic sound and picture printer. This award was presented at the Academy's seventh annual awards in 1934. The fourteenth Class III award went to Nathan Levinson, who was the Director of Sound Recording for Warner Brothers-First National Studios, for the method of intercutting variable density and variable area sound tracks to secure an increase in the effective volume range of sound recorded for motion pictures. Thomas T. Moulton and the United Artists Sound Department received the twenty-first Class III award in 1937 for the application to motion picture sound recording of volume indicators which have peak reading response and linear decibel scales. This type of volume indicator portrays with greater accuracy the form factor of an electrical wave. The forty-first Class III award went to Ray Wilkinson and the Paramount Studio Laboratory for pioneering in the use of and for the first practical application to release printing of fine grain positive

stock. Paul Zeff, S. J. Twining, and George Seid of the
Columbia Pictures Laboratory were given the sixtieth award
for the formula and for the application to production of a
simplified variable area sound negative developer. The
sixty-fourth award was given to Harland L. Baumbach and
Paramount West Coast Laboratory for an improved method for
the quantitative determination of hydroquinone and metol
photographic development. Herbert E. Britt received the
sixty-fifth Class III award for development and application
of formulas and equipment for producing cloud and smoke
effects. The seventy-second Class III award, presented
at the time of the nineteenth annual awards in 1946, went
to Harold Nye and Warners Electrical Department for development of the electronically controlled fire and gaslight
effect.[48]

In addition to the Class I, Class II, and Class III
scientific or technical awards the Academy gave out seven
special technical awards. The first was given at the tenth
annual awards in 1937 to W. Howard Greene for the color
photography of the film entitled A Star Is Born. The next
three were given at the eleventh annual awards in 1938.

---

[48]Ibid.

Oliver Marsh and Allen Davey received the second award for
the color cinematography of the film Sweethearts. The third
went for outstanding achievement in creating special photographic and sound effects in the Paramount production
Spawn of the North: special effects by Gordon Jennings,
assisted by Jan Domela, Dev Jennings, Irmin Roberts and
Art Smith; transparencies by Farciot Edouart, assisted by
Loyal Griggs; sound effects by Loren Ryder, assisted by
Harry Mills, Louis H. Mesenkop, and Walter Oberst. The
fourth special technical award was given to J. Arthur Ball
for his outstanding contributions to the advancement of
color in motion picture photography. The fifth special
technical award was given at the twelfth annual awards in
1939 to Fred Sersen and E. H. Hansen for the special effects in the film entitled The Rains Came. A sixth special
technical award was not given until the sixteenth year of
the annual awards in 1943. This award was presented to
George Pal for the development of novel methods and techniques in the production of the short subjects known as
Puppetoons. The seventh special technical award was given
at the eighteenth annual awards in 1945 to Republic Studios, Daniel J. Bloomberg and the Republic Sound Department
for the building of an outstanding musical scoring

auditorium which provided optimum recording conditions and combined all elements of acoustic and engineering design.[49]

Scientific or technical awards are basically different from other awards since they recognize achievements in the engineering field which must be based to some extent on prior accomplishments or developments. The Academy considers it only possible to recognize the individual or group whose work led to the final culmination of a project of current benefit to the motion picture industry. In so doing it is made clear that such recognition is without prejudice to the legal claims of anyone, and with no attempt to assess the originality of the accomplishment.

Technical Activities

As reviewed in Chapter III, pages 84-90 of this study, the technical activities of the Academy were accomplished under three groups: First, the Producers-Technicians Joint Committee; second, the Technical Bureau; and third, the Research Council. Working under the mechanism of these three groups, as one evolved into the other, the Academy made some of its most important and yet least known contributions to the motion picture industry.

---

[49]Ibid.

At the first meeting of the Producers-Technicians Joint Committee[50] on November 12, 1929, the committee adopted a policy of concentrating their work on problems of immediate and practical significance. They recognized there were many intriguing problems, such as the wide film that was being considered by some studios, which were too broad and involved complications beyond the scope of the committee. Three manageable problems suggested at this meeting were selected for their first tasks. The first was to devise a means of silencing the motion picture camera so it would not interfere with sound recording. The second was to arrive at the proper combination of set materials and stage construction which would enhance sound recording. The third was to arrive at the best method of silencing the arc lights.[51] Each of these will be discussed in some detail since they represent the very first work of the Academy in the solution of problems common to the industry, and whose solution constituted a real contribution to the

---

[50]The members of this committee were Irving Thalberg, M. C. Levee, Fred W. Beetson, J. A. Ball, Fred Pelton, J. T. Reed, Gerald Rackett, Sol Wurtzell, William Sistrom, Walter Stern, H. Keith Weeks, and Nugent H. Slaughter.

[51]Annual Report, Academy of Motion Picture Arts and Sciences, 1929, p. 51.

furtherance of motion picture technology.

  With the advent of sound, methods had to be developed by studios to keep the noise of the camera operation from microphones. Many studios started with inconvenient and cumbersome booths of an "ice-box"[52] construction. These shelters not only prevented free camera movement, but the hot stuffy shelters were most impractical for the camera operators. Gradually some of the cameramen began to use various types of covers which fit directly over the cameras. These early covers or blimps were never given adequate tests of efficiency in eliminating camera noise, and did not prevent noise interference with sound recording. The problem was to keep camera noises from the microphone without hindering the mobility of the camera. The special sub-committee established by the Academy's Producers-Technicians Joint Committee believed that by pooling studio experiences a new device or housing could be designed that would solve the problem. They made a survey of all studios, collecting complete data on booths, blimps, blankets, motors and covers, drive mechanisms, and camera-microphone distances. The different silencing devices and cameras

---

[52]Annual Report, Academy of Motion Picture Arts and Sciences, 1930, p. 17.

were then subjected to noise tests in the laboratories of

Electrical Research Products, Incorporated. The committee

found that variance in noise levels from uncovered cameras

was in itself a considerable factor in the problem. This

range was from 4 decibels to 20 decibels.[53] The silencing

efficiency of the different devices used for eliminating

noise in the cameras varied from 11 decibels to 21 decibels

for rigid devices, and from 1 decibel to 14 decibels for

semi-rigid coverings.[54] The best of the silencing devices

were re-tested to analyze the constructional details. As

a result of this investigation it was possible to prepare a

listing of fundamentals which should be embodied in all

silencing devices for cameras. This was then distributed

together with established standards for desired camera

noise tolerances varying from close-ups to location work,

a list of recommended materials for silencing devices, and

photographs of desirable types of construction.[55] In the

---

[53]Irving Thalberg, "Technical Activities of the
Academy of Motion Picture Arts and Sciences," Journal of
the Society of Motion Picture Engineers, XV, No. 1 (July,
1930), 3.

[54]Ibid.

[55]Annual Report, Academy of Motion Picture Arts and
Sciences, 1930, p. 17.

course of the investigation other industries had been contacted to see how similar sound damping problems had been
solved. For example, the Bell Telephone Laboratory development of a soldier's helmet for use in telephonic communication during combat, which had been most effective in keeping outside noises from the operator, was studied by the
committee. In addition to devices for silencing the camera,
considerable thought was given to the possibility of eliminating the sources of noise in the camera mechanism itself.
Mitchell Camera Corporation selected a camera with an 18
decibel noise level and was able to reduce its noise by 6
decibels.[56] A series of progress reports on the committee's
efforts was distributed to all interested studio personnel.

The classification of set materials according to
absorption characteristics required the cooperation of all
Hollywood studios. The Producers-Technicians Committee had
selected this project because it would not be practical for
one studio to undertake the necessary research. A sub-committee was appointed to concentrate on the problem of testing and classifying typical materials commonly used in set
construction for sound pictures. A questionnaire concerning

_____

[56]Unpublished material from the files of the Academy of Motion Picture Arts and Sciences.

the types of materials used was sent to all studios, and the
replies were carefully tabulated and analyzed to determine
what tests and experiments should be conducted.[57] No previous acoustical data could be used as tests had never been
made under motion picture studio conditions of operation.
The sub-committee not only determined what materials and
types of construction were generally used but also which
materials and construction were preferred on the basis of
low cost, ease of decoration and handling, and photographic
qualities. Ten of the most commonly used materials and
finishes were selected for testing under conditions similar
to studio practice. These ten were veneered flats papered
with crepe paper and hard wall paper; 7/16 inch Masonite
papered with crepe paper and flat oil paint; 7/16 inch
Celotex papered with crepe paper and one coat of water
paint; cast paper on burlap; cast stone on burlap;
and two different thicknesses of Zonolite plaster on
burlap covered chicken wire. Absorption coefficients at
typical frequencies were obtained for all ten of these
materials.[58] On the basis of these tests and the

---

[57]Annual Report, Academy of Motion Picture Arts and
Sciences, 1929, p. 30.

[58]Thalberg, loc. cit., p. 12.

subsequent interest of all studios, the sub-committee made
reverberation measurements in the studios themselves to
study the effects of open ceilings, of placement of microphones, and of the effect on the absorption-frequency curve
of bracing the sets by various spacings of the back-braces
of the set material. This latter test was the result of
questions related to the fact that all material first tested
had been rigidly braced for the prevention of resonance.
The emphasis was placed on actual studio practices due to
cost and operation techniques. Reports on all findings
were distributed to the studios.[59]

The high-frequency hum of arc lights, due to the
commutator ripple of the direct current generator, inter-
fered with sound recording. Studios using arc lights resorted to various devices to filter out the hum. A sub-
committee was appointed to investigate the problem, survey
the work done by studios, and report the best and most
feasible solution.[60] The studio survey revealed a wide
variation of design, efficiency, and expense of devices in

[59]Unpublished material from the files of the Academy of Motion Picture Arts and Sciences.

[60]Annual Report, Academy of Motion Picture Arts and
Sciences, 1930, pp. 17-18.

use. Actually there was very little quantitative information available on the commutator ripple, so oscillograph
records had to be obtained of each studio generating system.
Tests were conducted with the cooperation of the Los Angeles
Bureau of Power and Light which revealed the range of
ripple frequencies among the different generators. These
ranged from 750 to 3300 cycles with a maximum amplitude of
2.7 percent of the direct current voltage. Tests of the
studio devices revealed that one developed by Walter
Quinlan of Fox Film Corporation was sufficiently adapted
for the needs of all studios from the standpoint of efficiency and economy. It was not surprising to the sub-committee that Fox should have in use the best device since
that studio greatly preferred the use of arc lights.[61]
The survey showed that a filter for the ripple could be of
three different kinds: first, a condenser across the
mains; second, an inductance in the mains; and third, a
combination of the condenser across the mains and the inductance in the mains. The first type was considered to be
undesirable because its efficiency varied inversely with
the load. The second type was not considered sufficient

---

[61]Unpublished material from the files of the Academy of Motion Picture Arts and Sciences.

if efficiency at light as well as heavy loads was desired.
A large inductance coil was impracticable because of the
vast weight required, however small inductance coils placed
at the arcs themselves were practicable. The small inductance coils had small weight, volume, and heating loss.
Further they provided protection at each lamp which helped
keep feed-back noise out of the system. However, since
efficiency at light as well as heavy loads was required for
effective studio operations, it was deemed necessary to use
condensers across the mains in combination with small inductance coils. The device developed by Quinlan at Fox
was a type of electrolytic condenser of 1,000 microfarads
capacity which was able to withstand 150 volts. It was low
in cost, and would last for as long as ten months without
re-servicing if properly cared for.[62]

The advent of sound created another problem which
was of concern to studios, exchanges, and theatres. Since
there was no uniform standard for release prints each studio turned out prints with different leaders. As a result
the exchanges found the projectionists were cutting off
studio leaders, and substituting their own leaders. Even

---

[62]Ibid.

more disturbing was the practice of marking films with crude

and plainly visible changeover signals. The resultant muti-

lation of prints cost the motion picture industry thousands

of dollars. To solve this problem the Academy secured the

cooperation of the local organizations of projectionists,

cinematographers, and Society of Motion Picture Engineers.

Joint meetings resulted in the formation of a committee to

work out standards for approval by the industry. This com-

mittee conducted a thorough survey of current practices, and

after considerable experimentation arrived at a set of

meaningful specifications.[63] These standards included stan-

dard nomenclature for different types of prints as well as

for the units comprising each reel, standard inscription

for identification, standard synchronization marks, and a

standard method for change-over from reel to reel.[64] As a

result of the Academy's work, prints from the date of the

1931 productions were the first since the inception of

sound to be uniform throughout the industry, conforming to

specifications facilitating threading up, precision change-

---

[63]Academy Bulletin, No. XXVIII, January 29, 1930,
p. 3.

[64]Annual Report, Academy of Motion Picture Arts and
Sciences, 1930, p. 18.

over, and exact synchronization.

The non-standardization of apertures by cinematographers and projectionists led to image-loss with the new
sound-on-film. Projectionists, to achieve the old 3 x 4
proportion, inserted masks in the film gate which cut out
portions from the top and bottom of each frame. Then they
used a shorter focal length lens to enlarge the image so as
to fill the entire screen. Most cinematographers were not
aware of this practice, and therefore did not realize that
parts of their carefully composed pictures were lost. An
Academy sponsored committee made a nation-wide survey of
theatres, and a local survey of studios. As a result of the
evaluation of the data gathered the committee recommended
a temporary solution to be achieved by cinematographers
using sound-on-film methods. They were to make marks on the
camera ground glass equally spaced from top and bottom out-
lining a rectangle 0.620 by 0.835 inches in size, and com-
pose all pictures within the limits of this rectangle. In
addition all theatres which made a practice of re-establish-
ing the full screen proportions from sound-on-film pictures
were instructed to do so by use of an aperture whose size
would be 0.600 by 0.800 inches. This was to be on the basis
of projection on the level, the horizontal center of the

aperture coinciding with the horizontal center of the SMPE

Standard Aperture. The specifications were adopted by the

Standards Committee of the Society of Motion Picture Engi-

neers.[65]

The Academy noted that closer coordination was need-

ed between laboratory practices in the making of the master

negatives and release printing as accomplished both in the

East and West coast laboratories. A sub-committee appointed

to investigate the matter surveyed film processing, print-

ing, inspection, and shipment methods against the quality

of prints produced. After a detailed survey of all labora-

tory and exchange procedures the committee worked out stan-

dards based on the best observed practices. As part of the

program for gaining acceptance of these standards two re-

leases were prepared: the first contained characteristic

sounds that resulted from inefficient projection; and the

second those sounds resulting from improper laboratory pro-

cedures or exchange handling. As part of the final report

the committee included such information as proper methods

for storage and shipment of the negative; proper construc-

tion of laboratories; negative cleaning; dustproofing

---

[65]Unpublished material from the files of the Academy of Motion Pictures Arts and Sciences.

methods; care and maintenance of printing and processing
equipment; visual and aural methods for print inspection;
and recommended print handling techniques for exchanges.[66]

The relationship of screen illumination to print
density came under study as part of the overall Academy
desire to improve the quality of motion pictures shown to
the public. A special committee was formed to determine
minimum standards of illumination that would apply to the
majority of theatres. They recognized that economic factors would permit the top-quality theatres to exceed the
standards, and would also prevent the smallest theatres
from achieving them. Six representative theatres were
chosen in the Los Angeles area for the committee survey.
Illumination was measured at the screens with and without
films in the projector. The committee learned that the
same print shown in two theatres in which the length of
throw and screen illumination measurements were almost
equal appeared quite different. Additional tests revealed
that mirror lamps and high intensity lamps, which reflect
equal foot candles from the screen when projected through
a clear film gate, vary in the amount of light actually put

---

[66]Ibid.

through the film, and that this was due to brightness con-
trast. The committee prepared test reels which provided
density areas of measurable variances to enable accurate
appraisals of theatre projection facilities. The data thus
accumulated permitted production of prints with the desirable density, and correction of projection installations.[67]

The early work of the Academy under the Producers-
Technicians Committee and Technical Bureau proved the desirability of handling projects of mutual benefit to the entire
motion picture industry, and laid the ground floor for the
basic concepts under which the Research Council was to function. The Council undertook projects which involved investigation beyond the scope of an individual studio, and
which could be handled more economically and efficiently
in cooperative effort than by individual action. The technical activities of the Academy were to continue by committee action involving surveys, evaluation of data, dissemina-
tion of findings, and instigation of adoption of procedures
or standards by industry as appropriate.

One of the Academy's earliest benefits was to facil-
itate cooperation between the motion picture industry and

---

[67]Ibid.

the manufacturers of equipment. For example, the Academy
conducted a survey on behalf of the Bell & Howell Company
dealing with a proposed device to be attached to the camera
which would automatically print a "take" number on the side
of the film at regular intervals during the shooting of a
scene. The Academy sent 120 questionnaires to film editors,
cameramen, and sound men in both large and small studios.
The poll showed a two to one opinion that the device would
be valuable. Mr. H. McNabb, President of Bell & Howell
Company, wrote to the Academy:

> It is extremely gratifying to know that the Academy
> is successfully functioning in bringing about this
> long-wanted cooperation between producers and manu-
> facturers. [68]

Even relatively minor problems, if they involved
the entire industry, were proper and productive projects
for Academy sponsorship. For example, to avoid possible
halation from photographing white materials the studios
made use of such shades as yellow, blue, and pearl gray.
Actors found that very extensive wardrobes were required
since the studios varied as to the tints used. Many tests
of tints used resulted in the standardization of pearl
gray when a non-halation substitute for white was

---

[68] Academy Bulletin, No. XXIV, August 6, 1929, p. 4.

desired.[69]

The Technical Bureau of the Academy prepared a
glossary of terminology in 1930 which was badly needed since
so many new technical words and phrases from other fields
were being applied to motion pictures. The need had been
emphasized during the courses in sound given in 1929 when
terms from electrical engineering, radio, acoustics, and
physics were used by the instructors. The glossary drew
heavily on the definitions and glossaries published by the
Society of Motion Picture Engineers, the Institute of Radio
Engineers, the American Institute of Electrical Engineers,
and encyclopedias. Examples of the terms included are:

Aberration. In a lens, generally refers to Chromatic
Aberration. May also refer to Spherical Aberration,
a blurring of the focus due to the spherical shape
of the lens faces.

A-C Pick-Up. Undesirable sound in the recording
system--specifically, hum due to induction from
neighboring a-c circuits.

All Bottom. Sound in which low frequencies predomi-
nate.

Aeolight. Type of glow discharge tube which varies
the intensity of its emitted light in accordance with
small variations in the electric current flowing

[69]Research Council of the Academy of Motion Picture
Arts and Sciences, Technical Bulletin, December 23, 1932.

through it.   (First syllable pronounced to rhyme with day.)[70]

The technical activities of the Academy were continuous through the time period of this study. Not only were industry problems of major and minor significance to the motion picture industry undertaken but in some cases they were handled on a continuing basis as materials and techniques were improved or changed. For example, efforts were made to improve and maintain the quality of release prints. This required development and acceptance of standards for review projection equipment, sensitometry, densitometry, and other laboratory practices.

Detailed consideration of the total activity of the Academy in technical activities under the Producers-Technicians Joint Committee, Technical Bureau, and Research Council would require a separate study. This activity encompassed almost every facet of motion picture production from cameras through laboratory concerns to standardization of script formats.

Labor-Management

No single contribution of the Academy was to have

[70]"A Selected Glossary for the Motion Picture Technician," Compiled by the Technical Bureau, Academy of Motion Picture Arts and Sciences, 1930.

more controversial effects than those resulting from its
relationship to labor-management matters. At the time of
the Academy's conception the motion picture industry was
experiencing the same growing-pains in labor-management
relationships as were other industries throughout the
nation. It was therefore perfectly natural for Academy
members, who were representatives of both labor and management, to attempt to achieve harmony and cooperation in
this area.

The Academy's efforts were most productive during
the first six years of almost ten years of involvement with
labor-management problems. They began with its organization in 1927 and officially ceased in 1937 when the Academy
By-Laws were changed to reflect complete withdrawal from
the labor-management arena. This particular activity of
the Academy was to leave a record of both praise and
condemnation.

A Conciliation Committee was provided for in the
Constitution and By-Laws of the Academy at the very outset
of its organization. The founders believed that such a
committee would be effective in solving "controversies,
complaints, and grievances that may exist or arise between

the different branches or their members or between different

persons or companies engaged in motion picture production,

whether members or non-members[71] of the Academy."[72] The

membership of this committee was composed of one representa-

tive from each branch and was changed periodically during

its period of operation.[73]

The contributions of the Conciliation Committee with

regard to labor-management matters began at the time when

collective bargaining and collective negotiations were grad-

ually replacing the open-shop system.[74] Its actions were

watched with a great deal of interest by persons outside

---

[71]The Academy Secretary's report to the Board of
Directors on November 3, 1928 indicated that four-fifths of
the complaints originated from outside Academy membership.

[72]Academy of Motion Picture Arts and Sciences,
Information Bulletin, June 20, 1927.

[73]Conciliation committees were: 1927-28, John
Stahl, Milton Sills, Waldemar Young, L. B. Mayer, and Roy
Pomeroy; 1928-29, William Sistrom, J. T. Reed, Rod La
Rocque, Reginald Barker, and Tom Miranda; 1930-31, Lawrence
Grant, Reginald Barker, A. L. Rockett, J. T. Reed, and
Percy Heath; 1933, Percy Heath, J. T. Reed, Lawrence Grant,
Reginald Barker, and Albert Kaufman; 1934, J. A. Ball,
Lionel Atwill, John S. Robertson, M. E. Greenwood, and
Frank Woods.

[74]Murray Ross, Stars and Strikes (New York: Columbia University Press, 1941), p. 27.

the industry. For example, George J. Hatfield, United
States Attorney for the Northern District of California said
in a letter to the President of the Academy, Cecil B. de
Mille:

> The Conciliation Committee of the Academy is of spe-
> cial interest to me as a lawyer. For a great indus-
> try to have a Geneva of this kind for the impartial
> distribution of justice is, I believe, unique, and
> the experiment is worth watching.[75]

Complaints were first taken to the Executive Committee of
the branch to which the complainant belonged. If they
could not be reconciled at the branch level they were referred to the Conciliation Committee. The effectiveness of
the Committee was demonstrated in the satisfactory settlement of some 344 major cases involving actors and producers
over a four year period,[76] and some 63 disputes between
writers and producers over a six year period.[77] As William
C. de Mille stated:

> It is significant of the high purpose of the Academy
> and of the esteem in which it is held that the produc-
> ers have agreed to accept as final the decision of a
> committee which consists of four employees and only
> one employer.[78]

---

[75]Academy Bulletin XXVIII, January 29, 1930, p. 6.

[76]Ross, op. cit., pp. 38-39.

[77]Academy Bulletin XV, June 29, 1933, p. 6.

[78]Academy Bulletin XXIX, February 27, 1930, p. 1.

The Academy took direct action in the labor-management problem which occurred in the summer of 1927 when the
Producers' Association announced a 10 percent reduction in
salary for all non-union labor as an economy measure to offset rising production costs. The Academy Board of Directors[79] adopted a resolution on June 27, 1927 which stated
that the Academy was "not in sympathy with the movement recently instituted to decrease all salaries in excess of
$50.00 per week, without more specific consideration as to
the merits or demerits of each individual case."[80] The
resolution recommended suspending the proposed salary cut
until August 1, 1927 by which time it was hoped that ways
could be found for controlling production costs so that
salary reductions would not be necessary. The Producers'
Association agreed to the suspension until the first of
August, and the Academy branches of Technicians, Actors,
Writers, and Directors held separate meetings in which they
developed ideas for cutting production costs. The

---

[79]Douglas Fairbanks Sr., Conrad Nagel, Milton
Sills, Fred Niblo, Frank Lloyd, John Stahl, Mary Pickford,
L. B. Mayer, Joseph M. Schenck, Roy Pomeroy, Cedric Gibbons,
J. A. Ball, Jeannie Macpherson, Carey Wilson, and Joseph
Farnham.

[80]Academy Bulletin, No. 3, July 2, 1927, p. 2.

Directors' Branch, for example, proposed modifying production methods in their area of responsibility to cut down on negative costs. The ideas of the various branches were referred to the Academy's Producers' Branch prior to a series of conferences with the Producers' Association on the matter. The final conference took place at a dinner held at the Biltmore Hotel in Los Angeles on July 28, 1927 which was attended by more than 200 Academy members. The Producers' Association announced at this dinner that the proposed salary reduction was withdrawn.[81] During this period of time the Screen Writers' Guild and the Actors' Equity Association campaigned against the cut, and claimed the credit for it being rescinded on the basis of their own suggestions to the producers for cutting production costs.[82] About one year later Edwin Schallert, drama critic and editor for the Los Angeles Times, made this statement about the Academy's action in relation to the proposed salary cut by the Producers' Association:

> In its very beginning the organization entered the
> list in a critical situation that arose over a pro-
> posed ten percent cut in salaries around studio pro-
> duction forces, something over a year ago. During

---

[81]Academy Bulletin, No. 4, August 10, 1927, p. 1.

[82]Ross, op. cit., p. 55.

a series of conferences held at its insistence, it
succeeded in averting what promised to be virtual
chaos in pictures. Whether the Academy went outside
the bounds of its original plan in so doing has often
been a matter of debate, but the measures the organization took proved effective in this crisis.[83]

As covered in Chapter II, pages 22-23 of this study,
the screen actors, who had not encountered the abuses found
in the legitimate theatre, did not support Equity in its
attempts for a standard contract in 1924. This did not
mean that all screen actors had given up the possibility of
obtaining a standard contract, nor had Equity given up efforts to unionize the actors. Equity maintained an executive committee in Los Angeles with Conrad Nagel as Chairman.
It was therefore quite natural for Nagel to report progress
being made in the direction of a standard contract for free-
lance actors at the first organization meeting of the Actors' Branch of the Academy on June 2, 1927.[84] Progress on
the design of such a contract was to continue until early
1928 when Nagel announced that as chairman of the Equity's
executive committee in Los Angeles he was unable to negotiate the contract due to internal dissension in Equity,

---

[83]News item in Los Angeles Times, September 23,
1928.

[84]Academy Bulletin, No. 2, June 17, 1927, p. 3.

and in any event the producers had indicated a strong un-
willingness to deal with Equity.[85] In view of these matters, the Equity executive committee in Los Angeles, which
included Academy members Conrad Nagel and Hallam Cooley,
sought to negotiate the contract through the Academy. Nagel
believed he had a chance since "most actors were unconcerned
as to which organization represented them as long as they
had their way, and if the Academy could help them, they saw
no reason for clinging to Equity."[86] Equity dissolved the
Los Angeles executive committee because of this approach,
but agreed that the members could continue to negotiate a
contract as members of the Academy.[87] The members did continue to negotiate, and succeeded in obtaining a contract
approved by the Actors and Producers branches of the Academy and formally endorsed by the Board of Directors on
December 19, 1927. It became necessary to revise the contract on March 26, 1928 to clarify certain clauses, and
primarily to insert the provision that actor-producer disputes arising from the contract could be referred by either
party to the Academy Conciliation Committee.[88] This last

---

[85]Ross, op. cit., p. 28.

[86]Ibid.   [87]Ibid., pp. 28-29.

[88]Academy Bulletin, No. 9, April 2, 1928, p. 4.

provision merely formalized the use of the Conciliation
Committee since it had already been involved in settling
disputes arising from the original contract. Equity, which
had been critical of the contract, claimed the credit for
these changes.[89]

In January of 1928 the Writers' Branch of the Academy was praised by the Screen Writers' Guild for having
under preparation a standard contract for free-lance writers. Due to innovations in sound motion picture production,
such as the necessity for writing sound dialogue, negotiations for an acceptable contract became so complicated by
November of 1928 that the Guild requested work on the contract be suspended.[90] The Writers' Branch of the Academy
immediately discontinued their efforts awaiting clarifica-
tion of the situation.[91]

In late 1928 and early 1929 many stage players came
to Hollywood because of the promises of opportunities in
sound motion picture production. With increased numbers

---

[89] Ross, op. cit., pp. 38-39.

[90] Ibid., pp. 57-58.

[91] Academy of Motion Picture Arts and Sciences,
Secretary's Report at the Annual Meeting on November 3,
1928, p. 1.

of its members in Hollywood, Equity again sought to organize
the motion picture actors. They began with the announcement
that after June 5, 1929 Equity members could only accept
contracts approved by Equity, and were not to appear with
non-union actors. Equity members with contracts in force
on that date could continue to work, and even with non-
union actors, but then must meet Equity conditions upon contract renewal. Conrad Nagel arranged for a series of meetings between representatives of Equity and the producers.
However negotiations broke down, and when Ethel Barrymore,
Equity's First Vice President accused Frank Gillmore,
Equity's Executive Secretary, of misleading Equity members,
internal dissension resulted in the discontinuance of
Equity's attempts to organize the motion picture actors.
Equity then withdrew the June 5th regulation.[92] This left
the Actors' Branch of the Academy as the sole organization
to be of any value in the solution of such free-lance
actors' problems as obtaining a new standard contract.
Therefore, Robert Edeson, Chairman of the Actors' Branch
of the Academy, contacted the Producers' Association in
November of 1929 to negotiate for a revision to the

---

[92]Ross, op. cit., pp. 30-37.

standard contract for free-lance actors. A series of three
conferences were held in January of 1930 between representatives of a special actors' committee[93] and representatives[94] of the Producers' Association to work out the details for a new contract and the basic agreement for its administration.[95]

A significant point raised at the first conference
was the announcement by the producers that they would be
willing to adopt an eight-hour day with payments for
overtime for day-by-day engagements. By the third conference all details had been resolved except those pertaining
to a fifty-four hour week, which would impose complicated
methods for the recording and computing of work hours due
to the nature of motion picture production. Although the

[93]Representatives to the actors' committee were in-
creased during the period of the conferences and were final-
ly listed as: Conrad Nagel, Lloyd Hughes, Richard Tucker,
Robert Edeson, Wallace Beery, Lionel Belmore, Sam Hardy,
Jean Hersholt, Mitchell Lewis, Rod La Rocque, Lawrence
Grant, DeWitt Jennings, Ben Bard, Frank Reicher, Ben Lyons,
Monte Blue, Douglas Fairbanks, Jr., Helen Ware, Mae Murray,
Lois Wilson, William Courtenay, and Francis X. Bushman.

[94]Representatives to the producers' committee were
listed as: William Le Baron, Jack Warner, M. C. Levee,
Irving Thalberg, Sol Wurtzel, and Fred W. Beetson.

[95]Academy Bulletin, No. XXIX, February 27, 1930,
p. 1.

producers agreed to pay overtime this would not solve
the main concern of the actors which was to have adequate
rest periods. Therefore, the actors' committee proposed
that the fifty-four hour week be disregarded, and a
provision be inserted to give them a 12-hour rest period
after each day's work.[96] This was acceptable to the
producers, but the actors' committee decided the question
should be resolved at a general meeting of actors including
non-Academy members. This meeting was held on February 3
and was attended by more than 250 actors. The contract
was read to the group who unanimously adopted it including
the feature for a 12-hour rest period. They added the
proviso that if it did not work in practice after one
year the fifty-four hour week could be substituted at
the option of the actors' committee. The contract and
basic agreement were signed by several hundred actors
and endorsed by the Producers' Association on February 17,
and on February 21 the Academy Board of Directors accepted
the obligation for administering the new contract. This
responsibility included a provision in the contract

---

[96]According to Conrad Nagel this provision was the
result of his and Hallam Cooley's work, and was so successful an idea that it is retained today (1966) in the Screen
Actors' Guild contract.

for compulsory arbitration on any disputed points by an

Academy committee of five actors[97] with appeal to the Con-

ciliation Committee of the Academy.[98]

In 1931 the Writers' Branch[99] of the Academy re-

sumed efforts on a standard contract for free-lance writers.

By early 1932 it was decided by the writers and producers

that the diverse practices developed in the industry made

it advisable to leave all but three areas open to individ-

ual agreements between writers and producers. These three

areas were outlined in a code of practice on May 1, 1932.

"With the possible exception of the Academy Free-Lance

Actor Contract, this writer-producer code was given more

conscientious study and discussion than any other agreement

ever made between creative employees and the studios."[100]

The first of the three areas gave assurance that

any writer who worked without a contract for ten weeks or

---

[97]Known as the Actors' Adjustment Committee, it
was composed of DeWitt C. Jennings, Conrad Nagel, Jean
Hersholt, Claude Gillingwater, and Hallam Cooley.

[98]Academy Bulletin, No. XXIX, February 27, 1930,
p. 4.

[99]The Branch Executive Committee was composed of
Jack Cunningham, Paul Perez, John F. Goodrich, Winifred
Dunn, and Al Cohn.

[100]Ross, op. cit., p. 59.

longer at less than $500 per week was entitled to receive a week's notice on dismissal, and on the other hand should give a week's notice if he were to seek other employment. The second area prohibited producers from ordering preliminary or finished scripts on speculation, and required that writers be paid on delivery. The third area provided screen credit to writers.[101]

The Screen Writers' Guild referred to this code of practice as being a significant achievement between writers and producers, and Ross referred to it as a "great accomplishment."[102] However, "cooperation between writers and producers never reached the advanced stage attained by the actors."[103] Although the first area covered in the code was to become an accepted practice in the industry, it was found that the other two areas were difficult to deal with. Adherence to the code provisions during the depression became very lax with violations on part of both the writers and producers. Despite Academy efforts the writers resented the fact that they had never achieved a standard contract, or even a compulsory enforcement procedure for the

---

[101]Academy of Motion Picture Arts and Sciences, Special Bulletin, No. 44, Supplement No. 5, April 30, 1932.

[102]Ross, loc. cit.   [103]Ibid., p. 62.

code of practice. They were desirous of taking action free from the Academy where negligible gains had made them again distrust its motives.[104] The opportunity for the writers to make a strong move in this direction occurred with the bank-crisis in 1933.

The nation-wide bank moratorium of March 1933 was to be a major turning point in the Academy's efforts in the labor-management matters. As in industries all over the nation a sense of concern and worry for survival faced the motion picture industry. Production officials met in Hollywood to discuss the effects of the bank moratorium with the resultant expectation of facing studio shutdowns. Under the direction of controlling interests the studios proposed that all employees take a fifty percent paycut in an effort to keep production going. The studio locals of the International Alliance of Theatrical Stage Employees refused to take pay-cuts, and requested guarantees to pay when funds were available.[105] One studio announced to all employees that they would not receive any pay until bank funds were released. Another studio invoked a national emergency

---

[104]Ibid.

[105]The 1934 Motion Picture Almanac, p. 1110.

clause and suspended all contracts. Some employees announced that they would take pay-cuts if it would enable studios to continue in face of the financial crisis.[106]

In view of the confused crisis the Academy established a Salary Waiver Emergency Committee,[107] and recommended that salary waivers be limited to an eight week period. They "courageously proposed that the brunt of the loss be assumed by the high-salaried employees, including executives, directors, actors, and writers."[108] The Academy evolved a sliding scale based on the amount of individual earnings, and developed a plan for restoration of employee contributions and resumption of full salaries based on an audit[109] of the production companies books. As a result of this audit some companies were requested to re-

---

[106]Academy of Motion Picture Arts and Sciences, Emergency Bulletin, March 14, 1933, p. 1.

[107]The members of this committee were J. T. Reed, Lawrence Grant, Donald Crisp, B. P. Schulberg, Howard J. Green, and Lester Cowan. Alternate members were Karl Struss, Chester Morris, Robert E. O'Connor, Walter Huston, William K. Howard, and Oliver H. P. Garrett.

[108]Ross, op. cit., p. 46.

[109]Price, Waterhouse & Company was the firm selected, and has since been involved in the Academy Award proceedings.

store waivered salary funds and others told to return to
full salary prior to the end of the eight-week period.[110]
All companies did not agree with the findings of the Academy's Salary Waiver Emergency Committee,[111] and dissension
arose within the Academy. Conrad Nagel resigned as President of the Academy,[112] although retaining his membership,
and was replaced by J. T. Reed. The Academy, since it re-
lied on a spirit of cooperation and lacked any enforcement
mechanism, was not completely successful in having its recommendations carried out. This provided the impetus to
the actors and writers in their consideration of building
up independent craft unions that could resort to strikes to
enforce their demands. It is also quite possible that
unions looked better to Eastern management of motion picture studios since they could be bargained with at arm's
length rather than having their books opened and audited
with the results available to employees.

---

[110]Academy of Motion Picture Arts and Sciences,
Emergency Bulletin, No. 2, March, 1933, and No. 4, April,
1933.

[111]Metro-Goldwyn-Mayer and Warner Brothers did not
agree with the dates set by the Emergency Committee for resumption of full salaries.

[112]News item in New York Times, April 21, 1933.

Although the "Academy has done its best in a particularly bad situation"[113] many actors and writers were not
sure the Academy should have anything to do with their
labor-management problems. Consequently many actors began
to work more closely with the Screen Actors' Guild, and
many writers with the Screen Writers' Guild. At the same
time J. T. Reed took action to reorganize[114] the Academy
so that it could be more effective. However, the Academy
had scarcely begun to work out the reorganization, and to
recover from the effects of the salary-waiver problems,
when it became involved in new problems resulting from the
signing of the National Industrial Recovery Act on June 16,
1933.

Sol A. Rosenblatt, the NRA Deputy Administrator in
Charge of the Amusement Division, invited J. T. Reed to be
a member of the official code committee. Reed accepted
membership but abstained from signing the code so that the
Academy would be free to criticize any of its features, and
to allow for ratification of the code by the entire Academy
membership.[115] The preliminary code of fair practice

---

[113] Ross, op. cit., p. 47.

[114] Pages 43-48 of this study cover the pertinent
changes to the Constitution and By-Laws.

[115] Academy Bulletin, No. 24, August 24, 1933, p. 1.

contained three provisions concerning actors and writers
that were to be the basis of much controversy in the motion
picture industry. The first provision concerned anti-raiding, which made it illegal for one producer to take an employee away from another by salary increases or other means.
The second provision was to provide for establishment of a
Commission to register those agents with whom studios would
be allowed to deal. The third provision was to establish a
salary fixing board to control large salaries and to fine
any producer who offered unreasonable salaries.[116] Differences arose among Academy members "despite the Academy's
constant emphasis upon the need for unity during a period
of national emergency."[117] "The position of a peacemaker
during those turbulent days was not an enviable one."[118]

In July of 1933 the Academy established a code regarding agents which required clear statements of duties
and responsibilities, limited commissions to 10 percent,
and required statements of financial interest in all
agencies be filed with the Academy as a precaution against
producers who might have financial interests in agencies.

[116]Academy Bulletin, No. 25, August 28, 1933.

[117]Ross, op. cit., p. 99.   [118]Ibid., p. 100.

The code also provided for arbitration by the Academy of any disagreements involving the code or contracts with agents.[119] This code was included in the NRA preliminary code of fair practice together with all actors' and writers' agreements negotiated through the Academy. However the Academy, in review of the code, proposed several modifications. For example, it proposed that the executive committee of the actors and writers branches be permitted to negotiate changes in the contract forms before insertion into the code; that clauses inserted by producers along with the code concerning agents be eliminated since they put control into the hands of the studios, as in limiting the right of an employee to agent representation in such matters as salary and employment; and, to apply the anti-raiding provisions only to those making $1,000 or more per week or making $15,000 or more per picture with a contract for three or more pictures per year. In its criticism of the code the Academy could reach agreement with the producers only on the matter of the agents' code. Internal disagreements lingered within the Academy as the result of trying to work out all features. For example, as regards the anti-

---

[119]Academy Bulletin, No. 25, August 28, 1933.

raiding provision, the Actors' Branch opposed the other four
Academy branches in the matter of placing a thirty-day limit
on contract negotiations. The actors claimed this was too
short a period of time to work with a desirable contract.[120]
This internal dissension within the Academy came to public
attention at the hearings held on the Code for Fair Competition in Washington, D. C., in September 1933. Lionel Atwill
spoke for the Academy Actors' Branch opposing the other four
Academy branches on the anti-raiding provision. Statements
against the Academy were also made by the Actors' Equity
Association and the Screen Writers' Guild. J. T. Reed denied charges by Actors' Equity that the Academy was producer
controlled. He cited the Academy's objections to provisions
in the code as a sign of independence from producers. The
Screen Writers' Guild maintained that the vast majority of
motion picture writers were Guild members, and therefore the
Academy should not be used to represent the writers in the
code.[121] The net effect of all statements made at the hearings concerning the Academy was to exclude all points made
by the Academy from the NRA code drafted after the

---

[120] Academy Bulletin, No. 28, September 5, 1933, p. 3.

[121] NRA, Public Hearings on the Motion Picture Code.

hearing.[122] In this new code the producers incorporated a salary-fixing board to which the Academy took exception.[123] Despite this stand by the Academy, the actors and writers realized they would have to utilize their own unions to stop the NRA code since the Academy lacked the power to enforce its decisions. The Screen Writers' Guild and the Screen Actors' Guild worked together in having the provisions they objected to suspended by Executive Order and then permanently eliminated.[124] The two guilds collaborated very closely during the NRA period. They were served by the same legal counsel, and jointly published The Screen Guilds' Magazine.[125] The actors and writers concentrated their attention on strengthening their guilds rather than in supporting the Academy, which had been unable to eliminate the undesirable features in the code.

The guilds were still attempting in 1935 to have their requirements met under the NRA when it was declared unconstitutional. This ended the hopes of the guilds for

---

[122]Ross, op. cit., p. 103.

[123]Academy Bulletin, No. 30, September 26, 1933, p. 1.

[124]Ross, op. cit., pp. 104-106.

[125]Ibid., pp. 175-176.

achieving their ends under NRA controls.[126] From that time

until 1937 the Screen Actors' Guild worked for recognition

by the producers who finally gave in on May 15, 1937, and

granted the guild shop. The actors retained all concessions

under the guild shop that they had previously obtained under

the existing Academy contract, but now with the guarantee of

guild enforcement.[127] The Screen Playwrights, formed in

1936 by dissidents in the Screen Writers' Guild, also man-

aged to gain producers' recognition, and negotiated a con-

tract in April of 1937 which was essentially the same as the

old Academy's writer-producer contract except for the ad-

ministration.[128]

Thus, the movements of the guilds, which were

strictly labor organizations, following the NRA period pro-

vided a more direct and forceful machinery for dealing with

economic problems and the Academy withdrew entirely from

this area. The Academy, during its period of involvement

in labor-management affairs, was a unique example in a

major industry of an honorary professional organization in

which executives and employees met as individuals to

[126]Ibid., pp. 105-115. [127]Ibid., pp. 162-174.

[128]Ibid., pp. 178-181.

discuss and take action on their industry problems. It was

through the Academy that motion picture industry talent

groups first secured standardized contracts and codes of

practice, and had "their first taste of the fruits of col-

lective negotiation."[129] Although the Academy accumulated

considerable adverse criticism from the unions and guilds

because of its involvement in labor-management, once it

withdrew from that area and concentrated on technical re-

search and film awards "it was highly praised by the talent

unions."[130]

It is evident from the Academy's record that certain

factors precluded it from having a permanent role in labor-

management affairs. The five branches of the Academy were

representative of the five areas in motion picture produc-

tion. However, being a very limited and honorary group,

the Academy did not include in its membership a majority

of the total numbers working in the motion picture industry.

For many of the non-Academy members the influence of the

producers, even though they were only one branch of the

Academy, was suspect in any decision involving labor. The

inevitability of the development of strong specialized

[129] Ibid., p. 215.   [130] Ibid.

craft unions was a most significant factor, especially since the Academy lacked any enforcement mechanism to back up its decisions. Craft unions could resort to such techniques as strikes,[131] whereas the Academy had to rely entirely upon cooperative agreements.[132] Although this approach was to work amazingly well in many efforts, such as the actions of the Conciliation Committee, it proved ineffectual during the salary waiver disagreements in 1933. Despite the criticism levied on the Academy by the guilds and unions during its period of involvement in labor-management affairs its accomplishments cannot be overlooked. It is understandable that under the stresses of the situation the unions and guilds were unable to temper their criticism with an objective appraisal of what the Academy had been able to achieve in the labor-management area.

War Effort

One of the most important contributions of the Academy to the motion picture industry at the time of World War

---

[131] It was a threat to strike by the Actors' Guild in 1937 which resulted in the producers granting a guild shop.

[132] Conrad Nagel. Personal correspondence, January 21, 1966. Interview, January 30, 1966.

II was the establishment of a library of war films which had been produced by the governments of Great Britain, Canada, Russia, Mexico, and the United States. By agreement the films were to be shown on a strictly non-profit basis, and limited to studios, local military units, and the Academy membership. The prime purpose of the screenings was to provide the industry with authentic reference material, as well as to indicate availability of footage which could be used for background or insert.[133]

The Academy restricted its functions to securing the films, preparation of catalog listing for studio information, holding special screenings, and referring requests for the purchase of footage to the appropriate government agency. By 1943 the Academy had over 275 films, and by 1944 the number had increased to over 400. The films covered every aspect of the allied war effort and included mobilization, civilian defense, expansion of armament industry, participation by women in industry and the armed forces, rationing, war bond campaigns, military training, and combat scenes from battle fronts all over the world.[134]

---

[133]Academy of Motion Picture Arts and Sciences, "A Report--The Academy in Wartime," May 1, 1943.

[134]Academy War Film Library, Catalog of Prints, May, 1942-May, 1944.

Related to the war effort was the Academy's work for
the Army Signal Corps. For example, the Research Council of
the Academy had been requested by the Signal Corps of the
U. S. Army at the beginning of World War II to set up a special committee of twenty technicians to work out problems
of increasing the ease of operations of mobile photographic,
sound, projection, and laboratory equipment. One of the
most successful achievements of this committee was to design a new type of portable sound recording equipment. The
new design weighed only 250 pounds as compared to 750 pounds
for the older design with no loss of quality operation.[135]
This type of Academy activity, although of immediate benefit
to the Armed Services, was a contribution to the motion
picture industry in the improvement of equipment which had
uses outside the military.

Public Image Documentaries

In 1947 "Congressional committees began to institute investigations into 'un-American' activities in every
sphere of American life."[136] The House Un-American

[135]Academy of Motion Picture Arts and Sciences,
"A Report--The Academy in Wartime," May 1, 1943.

[136]Arthur Knight, The Liveliest Art (New York: The
Macmillan Company, 1957), p. 247.

Activities Committee was about to begin its hearings in
Hollywood in October of that year, when the Board of Governors of the Academy decided the public image of the motion
picture industry could be improved by the production of a
series of short documentaries on all major facets of film
production in Hollywood. They readily secured the cooperation of the Guilds, Unions, and Producers Association since
any benefits derived would be to the advantage of everyone
in the motion picture industry. Grant Leenhouts[137] was
selected by an advisory committee from the various organizations to be coordinator and producer for the series of
films. The series was to consist of twelve films designed
to acquaint the public with the real facts about the motion
picture industry and film production. Outlines for each
film were approved by the advisory committee prior to production. Made at various studios selected by Leenhouts the
costs for the first five were underwritten by the Producers
Association. The financial returns from the release of the
first five paid the costs for all twelve.[138] The films included such titles as: Let's Go to the Movies, Movies Are

---

[137]Motion picture writer, director, and producer.

[138]Grant Leenhouts, personal correspondence,
January, 1966.

Adventure, _The Art Director_, _Screen Actors_, _This Theatre and
You_, _The Screen Writer_, _Moments in Music_, _The Cinematogra-
pher_, and _The Costume Designer_. The series was completed in
September 1949, and all but four had been released by that
time to the public. In 1950 the entire series was distributed on 16mm to schools, libraries, and universities through
Teaching Film Custodians, Incorporated.[139] The effect of
these films on the public was considered to be favorable.[140]

Paper Print Reclamation

In 1947 the newly established Academy Foundation
sponsored a project to reclaim on film the paper print collection of old movies on file in the Library of Congress.
The Foundation had been organized to aid the cultural program of the Academy, and as a non-profit tax-exempt corporation could most appropriately make a very important contribution in this valuable historical project.[141]

There was no film copyright law until 1912, and the
first films produced in the United States from 1894 to 1912

[139] Academy of Motion Picture Arts and Sciences,
Report of the President, May 25, 1948.

[140] Leenhouts, _loc. cit_.

[141] Academy of Motion Picture Arts and Sciences,
Report of the President, May 25, 1948.

were copyrighted as photographs. The pioneers in the motion
picture industry printed every frame of film on rolls of
35mm photographic paper and deposited two copies of each
paper reel with the Copyright Office of the Library of Congress. This paper film collection was the only complete record of American picture production for that period. The
Congressional Library loaned the paper prints to the Academy
Foundation for re-conversion to safety film stock. The
paper film collection contained priceless Americana as well
as the only authentic history of the American film industry
from 1894 to 1912. Newsreels of the Boer War, the Spanish-
American War, Presidential Inaugurations, and views of
American cities at the turn of the century were all part of
these records. Conversion of the material to film involved
an expensive optical printing process. The first donation
came from the American Society of Cinematographers, and the
next from Eastman Kodak who gave the largest single contribution in the form of sufficient raw film stock for the
first year of conversion. Other companies, such as the
Thomas Edison Company, donated funds in support of the
project. The largest personal donations came from

Academy members.[142]

---

[142]Academy sponsorship of this project lasted for
two years, and then it was completed under funds appropriat-
ed as the result of a Congressional bill presented by
Senator Thomas H. Kuchel of California.

CHAPTER VI

SUMMARY AND CONCLUSIONS

Summary

The Academy of Motion Picture Arts and Sciences was founded in 1927 at a time when motion pictures were established as a powerful medium, and becoming recognized as an art form of the twentieth century. The silent film industry was reported to be the fourth largest industry in the United States, and was about to be revolutionized by the advent of sound. The motion picture industry was under constant public scrutiny, and the maintenance of a favorable public image was important. Harmonious internal relations in the labor-management field, and coordination in further development and standardization of equipment and techniques were important considerations in the industry.

The historical perspective of the founding period of the Academy is important in understanding the development, and achievements of the organization. America was

233

the strongest economic and military power in the world at the end of the first World War with a tradition of unbroken success in coping with any problem. Los Angeles had become a prime target for unionization, and by 1926 the motion picture industry had gone through three strikes before signing the first union agreement covering stagehands, carpenters, painters, electricians, and musicians. Equity had failed to establish standard contracts for screen actors or even to interest actors in forming a strong guild. The Screen Writers' Guild had failed to obtain a standard contract for writers. Motion picture production had become increasingly complex with the need for further development and standardization of technical developments and techniques. Public interest had declined in the silent film, and both the sound-on-film and sound-on-disc methods had made rapid progress. This was the period and the conditions which were reflected in the ideas of the founders of the Academy when they agreed to establish a professional society which might work toward the betterment of the motion picture industry.

The idea for establishing such an organization as tne Academy of Motion Picture Arts and Sciences came from Fred Niblo and Conrad Nagel. Their idea was enthusiastically endorsed by prominent individuals in the motion picture

industry, who together with Niblo and Nagel became the thirty-six founders of the Academy. Conceived by them to be an
exclusive, invitational, and honorary organization it was to
be composed of outstanding craftsmen from the technical,
acting, directing, producing, and writing fields of the motion picture industry. They believed such individuals could
work together within the framework of the professional society in cooperative achievement of mutually important goals.
The Academy of Motion Picture Arts and Sciences received
its charter under the laws of the State of California on
May 4, 1927.

The Academy's Constitution and By-Laws, as originally written and as subsequently changed over the years, contributed largely to the success of the organization by providing a solid framework for the organizational activities.
A considerable number of the changes were simply the natural result of organizational growth, but others were due to
external circumstances of the moment. Early attention giv-
en to countering unwarranted public criticism of the industry was dropped almost immediately, and never became a
major factor in Academy functions. The Board of Governors,
known as the Board of Directors until 1933, was maintained
over the years by effective rotational representation from

all Academy branches. The Officers of the Academy were
elected from this Board to provide continuity of understanding and purpose in management of Academy plans and programs.
In 1933 election of Officers was opened to all Academy members rather than just the Board to offset criticism that
management was concentrated in the hands of a few individuals. In 1946 the Academy returned to the system of election of Officers from the Board to provide the desired continuity in understanding of management problems.

The physical facilities of the Academy were planned
and improved over the years in order to be more beneficial
to the members in carrying out established functions. The
Academy published valuable material for the motion picture
industry in the form of reference books on sound, technical
bulletins, credit data bulletins, and directories for actors and actresses.

Membership began with slightly over 200 men and
women growing to over 800 by 1932, and then beginning a
gradual decline after the bank-crisis period in 1933. This
decline, particularly among actors and writers who were
concentrating on strengthening their guilds, continued
through the late thirties until it reached the 1929 membership level of over 400 members. Membership then began to

increase until there were over 1,600 members by 1947. Membership, over the years, was by invitation only, and required distinctive achievement in one of the various branches of the industry as measured by persons in the Academy of equal competence in the same fields. The various categories of membership changed over the years in reflection of the industry's and Academy's growth. Beginning with the original five branches of actors, producers, writers, directors, and technicians the Academy grew to twelve branches by 1947. These twelve branches were Art Directors, Film Editors, Music, Cinematographers, Public Relations, Short Subjects, Actors, Writers, Directors, Producers, Sound, and Executives. The replacement of the Technicians' Branch with its separate sections as independent branches came as a natural result of the growth and importance of specialization in the motion picture industry.

Awards of Merit were designed to reward and stimulate creativity by giving public credit to outstanding achievements in the motion picture industry as determined by persons directly involved in the same field. The methods of selection and kinds of awards changed continually to reflect the growth and interplay of the various elements of the art and science of motion pictures. With the

membership decline in the late thirties the Academy asked
the guilds and unions in 1937 to participate in the nominations and final voting to provide a more representative selection process. By 1946 the Academy membership had grown
to over a thousand and the final vote was reserved for
Academy members.

The Academy made many contributions to education
over the years, assisting or working with formalized
schools and colleges, Academy members, personnel of the motion picture industry, and the armed forces. The Academy
established extensive cooperative efforts with the University of Southern California; out of this background the
University of Southern California, through its Cinema Department, became the foremost university in the country in
training and education in the field of motion picture photography. Academy contacts influenced the creation of a
Theatre Arts Department within the University of California
at Los Angeles, offering a motion picture curriculum. Over
the years the Academy furnished a great deal of material and
assistance to educational institutions and to individuals
on a world-wide basis. The early schools in sound for members of the motion picture industry were a major contribution in education to an industry faced with such a major

technical change and having little or no knowledge of the
subject. Academy members were provided with special presentations and facilities for self-improvement through mutual
exchange of ideas and concepts. The special training provided to selected members of the Army Signal Corps was
largely responsible for the ultimate success of the Army
training film program.

The Academy's contributions to the motion picture
industry itself were both direct and indirect. The assistance given to the public and special groups outside the
profession created good-will for the motion picture industry. Academy support enhanced the success of projects and
beneficial movements both for the public and the industry.
The Academy enjoyed a degree of success and failure in the
labor-management area until 1937 when it withdrew officially from such matters. This involvement in labor-management
problems was to leave a record of criticism against the
Academy. However, the Academy did make many valuable contributions in this area. A standard contract for free-
lance actors was developed and modified. A Conciliation
Committee was created which successfully settled more than
400 disputes for both Academy and non-Academy members. The
Academy was successful in having a salary reduction

withdrawn by the producers in June of 1927. A code of practice for writers was developed; however, the Academy was
never to be as successful in behalf of the writers as with
the actors. The nation-wide bank moratorium in 1933 was to
be a major turning point in the Academy's efforts in labor-
management matters. Lacking any enforcement mechanism the
Academy was unable to be completely effective during this
period of crisis. The Academy was also ineffective in
attempts to remove undesirable features from the NRA code,
and to encourage membership support of the Academy through
reorganization. During this period the actors and writers
concentrated on strengthening their guilds rather than attempting to cooperate with the Academy. The Screen Actors
Guild achieved producer recognition and a guild shop in May
of 1937 by threatening to strike. Dissidents from the
Screen Writers' Guild, who had formed the Screen Playwrights, managed to negotiate a contract in April of 1937
with producers. The development of these more effective
mechanisms for dealing with labor problems resulted in the
Academy's official withdrawal from the labor-management
arena. Criticism of the Academy by the guilds and unions
then turned to praise for its efforts in matters concerning
merit awards and technical developments. Despite the

accumulated criticism against the Academy it is a matter of
record that the talent groups first secured standardized
contracts and codes of practice, and experienced the benefits of collective negotiation through the Academy. During
this period of involvement in labor-management affairs the
Academy was a unique example of an honorary professional organization in which executives and employees met as individuals to discuss and take cooperative action on mutual problems in their industry.

The Academy sponsored corrective action when the
motion picture industry faced a loss of revenue as sound
created problems for the foreign market. Sponsorship of a
still photographic contest, and subsequent world-wide exhibits of the contest stills, was to benefit the industry in
the form of institutional publicity. Academy Awards of
Merit have been a special contribution to the motion picture industry. The resulting publicity has increased public attention to the entertainment films, and provided recognition within the industry to outstanding achievements
by individuals. The scientific or technical awards reflect
milestones in the historical development of the industry.
Barely known outside the industry, they have served as a
stimulus to competitive creative effort. Even less known

has been the Academy contribution to technical advancements through the successive mechanism of the Producers-Technicians Joint Committee, the Technical Bureau, and the Research Council. The manifold problems posed by the advent of sound were to be the primary targets of these activities. Solutions to the problems of camera silencing, acoustics of set materials, silencing of arc lights, standardization of release prints, coordination of laboratory and projection equipment and techniques to improve the final print appearing before the public were provided the entire industry as the result of Academy efforts. Nearly every facet of motion picture production was given consideration in the technical activities of the Academy.

World War II provided the Academy with the occasion to assist both industry and the armed forces. The war film library and connections with appropriate governmental agencies maintained by the Academy for members of the motion picture industry were of great importance. In addition, the Academy pioneered in the field of industrial research in support of the armed forces; a classic example was the design and development of a compact sound recorder of smaller size and lesser weight to meet Signal Corps requirements.

In the postwar years, the Academy sponsored the production of a series of documentaries on the motion picture industry which were designed to improve the public image of the industry. This was undertaken at a time when the public attention was focused on the industry in light of the forthcoming investigations by the House Un-American Activities Committee. This year also saw the beginning of a two-year sponsorship by the Academy of the reclamation of the paper print collection of early motion pictures stored in the Library of Congress. This project was of real significance in preserving and making available on 16mm film to historians the earliest American motion pictures from the 1894-1912 period.

Conclusions

This study has revealed that the Academy of Motion Picture Arts and Sciences, little known except for its Awards of Merit, parallelled, reflected, and contributed to the advancement of the American motion picture industry ever since the end of the silent film era. Before the Academy was founded there had been no mechanism for personnel of the motion picture production elements to engage in harmonious and cooperative action for the benefit of the

industry. In an era when heedless economic competition was
the hallmark of American progress, it is no small tribute
to the original founders that their vision and early efforts
should have resulted in the creation of a professional society which accomplished so much for the motion picture industry.

As a result of this historical study of the Academy,
the questions proposed initially can be answered as follows:

1. Why did the founders conceive of the need for a
   professional society composed of members of the
   motion picture industry?

As products of the times in America the founders
recognized that their industry needed an organization which
could bring about harmonious and concerted action toward
self-improvement and that such an organization was better
self-generated than imposed from the outside.

2. Who were the founders, and were they truly representative of the entire motion picture industry?

The founders were all pioneers in the motion picture industry, leaders in their particular field, and from
all main elements of production. These elements were writing, production, acting, editing, directing, cinematography,

and executive. Out of these elements the original five
branches were designated as representing actors, writers,
directors, producers, and technicians.

3. What were the purposes, aims, and goals of the
Academy, and how did they develop over the
years?

The purposes, aims, and goals were stated by the
founders at the time of organization. The Academy record
of accomplishments and contributions has been remarkably
faithful to the intentions of the founders. It should be
noted that the Academy never failed to step aside in favor
of any organization more appropriate to carry out a particular aim once action had indeed been initiated. The Academy's withdrawal from economic matters in favor of the
unions and guilds is a good example of this Academy policy.

4. What were the contributions of the Academy
to education and to the motion picture industry?

As outlined in Chapter IV, the Academy sponsored a
program of higher education to promote its own profession,
and contributed techniques and resources to all phases of
education. This sponsorship, and the working relations
arising therefrom, were significant factors in the development of the Cinema Department at the University of Southern

California and the Theatre Arts Department at the University
of California at Los Angeles. Although this particular contribution did not achieve the public notice accorded Awards
for Merit it may well prove to be its most important contribution. As outlined in Chapter V the contributions to the
motion picture industry also varied in scope, and were most
significant in stimulating morale, establishing a sense of
professional identity, and promoting cooperative effort in
solution of technical problems.

>   5. What factors have led to the continued existence
>   of the Academy as a non-profit organization
>   which is not an official spokesman for the
>   industry?

The basic organizational concepts and cooperative
achievements, particularly those related to technical activities and Awards of Merit, have resulted in its continuance
and final acceptance by outstanding personnel in the motion
picture industry as being an important and worthwhile honorary professional organization.

Suggestions for Further Studies

A valuable research project would be a detailed
study of the involvement of the Academy and its members in

labor-management affairs, and the effects of this involvement on unions and guilds.

Another valuable research project would be a detailed study of the total activity of the Academy in technical matters under the Producers-Technicians Joint Committee, Technical Bureau, and Research Council.

BIBLIOGRAPHY

BIBLIOGRAPHY

Books

Academy of Motion Picture Arts and Sciences. Motion Picture Sound Engineering. Princeton: D. Van Nostrand Company, 1938.

Arnheim, Rudolph. Film as Art. Berkeley and Los Angeles: University of California Press, 1957.

Balazs, Bela. Theory of Film. New York: Roy Publishers, 1953.

Barnouw, Erik. Mass Communication Television, Radio, Film, Press. New York: Rinehart and Company, Inc., 1956.

Butts, R. Freeman, and Cremin, Lawrence A. A History of Education in American Culture. New York: Henry Holt and Company, 1953.

Clark, Henry. Academy Award Diary 1928-1955. New York: Pageant Press, Inc., 1959.

Cowan, Lester (ed.). Recording Sound for Motion Pictures. New York and London: McGraw-Hill Company, Inc., 1931.

Crowther, Bosley. Hollywood Rajah. New York: Dell Publishing Company, Inc., 1960.

Eisenstein, Sergei M. Film Form. New York: Harcourt, Brace & Co., 1949.

_____. The Film Sense. New York: Harcourt, Brace & Co., 1942.

249

Elliot, Godfrey M. (ed.). Film and Education. New York: Philosophical Library, Inc., 1948.

Emery, Edwin, Ault, Phillip H., and Agee, Warren K. Introduction to Mass Communications. New York: Dodd, Mead Company, 1960.

Faulkner, Harold Underwood. American Political and Social History. New York: Appleton-Century-Crofts, Inc., 1952.

Fite, Gilbert C., and Reese, Jim E. An Economic History of the United States. Boston: Houghton Mifflin Company, 1959.

Green, Fitzhugh. The Film Finds Its Tongue. New York: G. P. Putnam's Sons, 1929.

Hays, Will H. The Memoirs of Will H. Hays. Garden City, New York: Doubleday & Company, Inc., 1955.

Hughes, Robert (ed.). Film: Book I. New York: Grove Press, Inc., 1959.

Jacobs, Lewis. Introduction to the Art of the Movies. New York: The Noonday Press, 1960.

_____ The Rise of the American Film. New York: Harcourt, Brace & Company, 1939.

Jobes, Gertrude. Motion Picture Empire. Hamden, Connecticut: Archon Books, 1966.

Kennedy, Joseph P. (ed.). The Story of the Films. New York: A. W. Shaw Company, 1927.

Knight, Arthur. The Liveliest Art. New York: Macmillan Company, 1957.

Lazarsfeld, Paul F., and Berelson, Bernard (ed.). The Effects of Mass Communication. Glencoe, Illinois: The Free Press, 1960.

Likeness, George C. The Oscar People. Mendota, Illinois: The Wayside Press, 1965.

Lindsay, Vachel. The Art of the Moving Picture. New York: The Macmillan Company, 1915.

MacGowan, Kenneth. Behind the Screen. New York: Delacorte Press, 1965.

Manvell, Roger. Film. Rev.ed. London: Hazell Watson and Viney, Ltd., 1950.

Michael, Paul. The Academy Awards: A Pictorial History. New York: The Bobbs-Merrill Company, Inc., 1964.

Moley, Raymond. The Hays Office. New York: The Bobbs-Merrill Company, Inc., 1945.

Nicoll, Allardyce. Film and Theatre. New York: Thomas Y. Crowell Company, 1936.

Osborne, Robert. Academy Awards Illustrated. Hollywood: Marvin Miller Enterprises, 1965.

Palmer, Edwin O. History of Hollywood. Hollywood: Arthur H. Cawston, Publisher, 1937.

Ramsaye, Terry. A Million and One Nights. New York: Simon & Schuster, 1926.

Ross, Murray. Stars and Strikes. New York: Columbia University Press, 1941.

Rosten, Leo Calvin. Hollywood. New York: Harcourt, Brace & Company, 1941.

Rotha, Paul, and Griffith, Richard. The Film Till Now. New York: Funk & Wagnalls, 1949.

Rugg, H. Social Foundations of Education. New York: Prentice-Hall, Inc., 1955.

Spottiswoode, Raymond. Film and Its Techniques. Berkeley and Los Angeles: University of California Press, 1959.

_____. A Grammar of the Film. Berkeley and Los Angeles: University of California Press, 1950.

Wiseman, Thomas. Cinema. New York: A. S. Barnes and Company, 1965.

Wollenberg, H. H. Anatomy of the Film. Cambridge: Maryland, 1947.

Publications of Learned Societies and Other Organizations

Abbott, A. M. "Equipment Used for Motion Pictures," The Annals of the American Academy of Political and Social Science, CXXVIII (November, 1926), 34-45.

Cochran, Blake. "Films on War and American Policy," American Council on Education Studies, October, 1940, pp. 1-63.

Dale, Edgar, and Ramseyer, Lloyd L. "Teaching with Motion Pictures," American Council on Education Studies, Series II, No. 2 (April, 1937), pp. 1-59.

Equity (New York), 1915-1941.

Gallez, Douglas W. "Training Army Personnel for Motion Pictures and Television," Journal of the Society of Motion Picture and Television Engineers, LXXII (April, 1963), 281-283.

Gledhill, Donald. "The Motion Picture Academy, A Cooperative in Hollywood," Journal of Educational Sociology, XIII, No. 5 (January, 1940), 268-273.

Hickman, K. C. D. "Hollywood and the Motion Picture Engineers," Transactions of the Society of Motion Picture Engineers, XI (April, 1927), 34.

Kent, Sidney R. "The Motion Picture of Tomorrow," The Annals of the American Academy of Political and Social Science, CXXVIII (November, 1926), 30-33.

Screen Actor (Hollywood, California), 1934-1947. (Absorbed Screen Player, Screen Guilds' Magazine, Screen Guild Magazine, Official Bulletin, and The Actor, 1934-1940.)

Society of Motion Picture Engineers. Journal of the Society of Motion Picture Engineers (Washington, D. C.), 1927-1947. (Supersedes Transactions of the Society of Motion Picture Engineers, 1916-1929.)

Thalberg, Irving. "Technical Activities of the Academy of Motion Picture Arts and Sciences," Journal of the Society of Motion Picture Engineers, XV, No. 1 (July, 1930), 3-16.

Articles and Periodicals

Beaton, Welford. "Industry Fashioning Weapon of Defense," The Film Spectator, III, No. 7 (May 28, 1927), 3.

_____. "Is Entitled to Support of All," The Film Spectator, III, No. 7 (May 28, 1927), 4.

Daily Variety (Hollywood, California), 1936-1947.

Film Daily (New York), 1929-1947.

Film Daily Year Book. New York: Worlds Films and Film Folk, Inc., 1926-1947.

Hollywood Reporter. 1935-1947.

International Motion Picture Almanac. New York: Quigley Publications, 1929-1947.

Levinson, André. "The Nature of the Cinema," Theatre Arts Monthly, XIII, No. 9 (September, 1929), 684-693.

Los Angeles Times. 1926-1929.

Menzies, Cameron. "Cinema Design," Theatre Arts Monthly, XIII, No. 9 (September, 1929), 676-683.

Motion Picture Daily (New York), 1934-1947.

Pacific Bindery Talk, XIII, No. 2 (October, 1940).

Motion Picture Herald (New York), 1931-1947.

New York Times. 1926-1947.

Ramsaye, Terry. "The Industry," Theatre Arts Monthly, XIII, No. 9 (September, 1929), 656-663.

"Technical Experts to Set Up Theatre Standards," Hollywood Filmograph, IX, No. 34 (August 24, 1929), 21.

Variety (New York), 1926-1947.

Public Documents

U. S. National Recovery Administration. Code of Fair Competition for the Motion Picture Industry. Washington, D. C.: U. S. Government Printing Office, 1933.

_____. Public Hearings on the Motion Picture Code. September, 1933.

Unpublished Material

Academy of Motion Picture Arts and Sciences. "Annual Report." 1929-1930, 1941.

_____. "Bulletin." 1927-1935.

_____. "News Letter." 1945-1947.

_____. "Report of the President, 1949-1950."

_____. "A Report--The Academy in Wartime," May 1, 1943.

_____. "Producers-Technicians Joint Committee and Technical Bureau Reports." 1928-1931.

_____. "Research Council Technical Bulletin." 1932-1947.

_____. "Articles of Incorporation." March 19, 1927.

_____. "Invitation to Organization Banquet." May, 1927.

————. "Verbatim Transcript of Organization Banquet."
    May, 1927.

"Films for Classroom Use," Teaching Film Custodians, Inc.,
    November, 1946.

"Introduction to the Photoplay," Copyright University of
    Southern California and the Academy of Motion Picture
    Arts and Sciences, 1929. (Mimeographed.)

Interviews and Personal Correspondence

Brown, Sam E. Assistant Executive Director, Academy of
    Motion Picture Arts and Sciences. Personal interviews,
    1963 and 1966. Personal correspondence, January 31,
    1966.

Franklin, Elizabeth. Former Librarian, Academy of Motion
    Picture Arts and Sciences. Personal interviews, 1963.

Gledhill, Donald G. Former Executive Secretary, Academy of
    Motion Picture Arts and Sciences. Personal interviews,
    1965. Personal correspondence, December 5, 1965.

Herrick, Margaret. Executive Director, Academy of Motion
    Picture Arts and Sciences. Personal interviews, 1963.

Leenhouts, Grant. Writer, director, and producer. Personal
    correspondence, January, 1966.

Levee, Michael C. One of the founders and third President
    of the Academy of Motion Picture Arts and Sciences.
    Personal correspondence and taped interview, January,
    1966.

Mitchell, Gordon S. Former Manager, Research Council,
    Academy of Motion Picture Arts and Sciences. Personal
    correspondence, January 19, 1966.

Nagel, Conrad. One of the founders and fourth President of
    the Academy of Motion Picture Arts and Sciences.
    Personal correspondence, January 24, 1966. Interview,
    January 30, 1966.

APPENDIX

APPENDIX

I. FOUNDERS OF THE ACADEMY OF MOTION PICTURE ARTS AND SCIENCES

Ball, J. A.

Barthelmess, Richard

Beetson, Fred

Christie, Charles

Cohen, George

de Mille, Cecil B.

Fairbanks, Douglas, Sr.

Farnham, Joseph W.

Gibbons, Cedric

Glazer, Benjamin

Grauman, Sid

Hoffman, Milton

Holt, Jack

King, Henry

Lasky, Jesse

Levee, M. C.

Lloyd, Frank

Lloyd, Harold

Loeb, Edwin

Macpherson, Jeanie

Mayer, Louis B.

Meredyth, Bess

Nagel, Conrad

Niblo, Fred

Pickford, Mary

Pomeroy, Roy

Rapf, Harry

Schenck, Joseph M.

Sills, Milton

Stahl, John

Thalberg, Irving G.

Walsh, Raoul

Warner, Harry

Warner, Jack

Wilson, Carey

Woods, Frank

II. FIRST OFFICERS AND BOARD OF DIRECTORS OF THE ACADEMY OF MOTION PICTURE ARTS AND SCIENCES

Officers of the Academy

Douglas Fairbanks Sr., President

Fred Niblo, Vice President

M. C. Levee, Treasurer

Frank Woods, Secretary

Board of Directors

For the Actors

Douglas Fairbanks Sr., Conrad Nagel, Milton Sills

For the Directors

Fred Niblo, Frank Lloyd, John Stahl

For the Producers

Mary Pickford, Louis B. Mayer, Joseph M. Schenck

For the Technicians

Roy Pomeroy, Cedric Gibbons, J. A. Ball

For the Writers

Jeanie Macpherson, Carey Wilson, Joseph Farnham

III. TEXT OF EDISON'S REMARKS IN A TALKING PICTURE REEL
SENT TO THE ACADEMY OF MOTION PICTURE ARTS AND SCIENCES
FOR THEIR FOURTH ANNUAL MEETING ON NOVEMBER 5, 1930

Ladies and Gentlemen:

The motion picture came into existence as a result of technical pioneering in which I am happy to have played a part. From the date of its birth, its development has been continuous. It gives me great pleasure to know that your Academy, whose members are devoting their lives to this great new art and industry, is taking from the hands of motion pioneers, the torch of technical and artistic progress. I am happy to have played a part in the technical pioneering which brought the motion picture into existence.

I am happy also to be the first honorary member of your society. To you active members of the Academy of Motion Picture Arts and Sciences I wish every success in your work, and I congratulate those who, through their outstanding contribution, have earned the laurels you are this evening bestowing.

No clear-minded individual could fail to observe during the past decade, the tremendous advance of the screen, artistic and otherwise, the higher standards which the producers have developed, the larger spirit of public service, the increased devotion to the realities of life and art, the wide open door to technical development.

There are many who would humble the art of the screen and its service to mankind by making it conform to their narrow personal standards. The screen is still subject to misrepresentation from those who are living in the past and have not viewed the continuous development of this great medium of communication and expression, but to the alert mind, the progress of the screen should be self-evident. Through this progress, it is rising above the criticism of those who stand here aloof and it is coming ever nearer to the attainment of those goals of art and science and human service which fill the minds of its active and responsible leaders.

IV.   LECTURE SCHEDULE FOR "INTRODUCTION

TO THE PHOTOPLAY"

Introduction and Plan of the Course
    Dr. Karl T. Waugh

Photoplay Appreciation
    Douglas Fairbanks, Sr.

Photoplay and the University
    Dr. Rufus B. von KleinSmid

Scientific Foundations
    J. A. Ball

Early History
    Commodore J. Stuart Blackton

Growth and Development
    David Wark Griffith
    Frank Woods

The Silent Photoplay
    Ernst Lubitsch

The Photoplay with Sound and Voice
    Benjamin Glazer

The Modern Photoplay
    Irving Thalberg

The Story
    Clara Beranger

The Actor's Art
    Milton Sills

260

Pictorial Beauty in the Photoplay
    W. C. Menzies

Commercial Requirements
    M. C. Levee

Principles of Criticism
    Edwin Shallert

Social Utility of the Photoplay
    Dr. Karl T. Waugh

The Photoplay and Aesthetic Culture in the World
    Dr. J. A. Leighton

Control of the Screen
    Professor Emory S. Bogardus

Future of the Photoplay
    William C. de Mille

V. KEY PAID STAFF DIRECTORS OF THE ACADEMY OF

MOTION PICTURE ARTS AND SCIENCES

1927-1931   Frank Woods (Title was Secretary.)

1931-1933   Lester Cowan (Title was changed to Executive
             Secretary.)

1933-1942   Donald Gledhill (Title was Executive Secre-
             tary.)

1942-   Margaret Herrick (Title was changed to
             Executive Director.)

262

The Arno Press Cinema Program

THE LITERATURE OF CINEMA

Series I & II

Agate, James. **Around Cinemas.** 1946.

Agate, James. **Around Cinemas.** (Second Series). 1948.

American Academy of Political and Social Science. **The Motion Picture in Its Economic and Social Aspects,** edited by Clyde L. King. **The Motion Picture Industry,** edited by Gordon S. Watkins. *The Annals,* November, 1926/1927.

L'Art Cinematographique, Nos. 1-8. 1926-1931.

Balcon, Michael, Ernest Lindgren, Forsyth Hardy and Roger Manvell. **Twenty Years of British Film, 1925-1945.** 1947.

Bardèche, Maurice and Robert Brasillach. **The History of Motion Pictures,** edited by Iris Barry. 1938.

Benoit-Levy, Jean. **The Art of the Motion Picture.** 1946.

Blumer, Herbert. **Movies and Conduct.** 1933.

Blumer, Herbert and Philip M. Hauser. **Movies, Delinquency, and Crime.** 1933.

Buckle, Gerard Fort. **The Mind and the Film.** 1926.

Carter, Huntly. **The New Spirit in the Cinema.** 1930.

Carter, Huntly. **The New Spirit in the Russian Theatre, 1917-1928.** 1929.

Carter, Huntly. **The New Theatre and Cinema of Soviet Russia.** 1924.

Charters, W. W. **Motion Pictures and Youth.** 1933.

Cinema Commission of Inquiry. **The Cinema: Its Present Position and Future Possibilities.** 1917.

Dale, Edgar. **Children's Attendance at Motion Pictures.** Dysinger, Wendell S. and Christian A. Ruckmick. **The Emotional Responses of Children to the Motion Picture Situation.** 1935.

Dale, Edgar. **The Content of Motion Pictures.** 1935.

Dale, Edgar. **How to Appreciate Motion Pictures.** 1937.

Dale, Edgar, Fannie W. Dunn, Charles F. Hoban, Jr., and Etta Schneider. **Motion Pictures in Education: A Summary of the Literature.** 1938.

Davy, Charles. **Footnotes to the Film.** 1938.

Dickinson, Thorold and Catherine De la Roche. **Soviet Cinema.** 1948.

Dickson, W. K. L., and Antonia Dickson. **History of the Kinetograph, Kinetoscope and Kinetophonograph.** 1895.

Forman, Henry James. **Our Movie Made Children.** 1935.

Freeburg, Victor Oscar. **The Art of Photoplay Making.** 1918.

Freeburg, Victor Oscar. **Pictorial Beauty on the Screen.** 1923.

Hall, Hal, editor. **Cinematographic Annual,** 2 vols. 1930/1931.

Hampton, Benjamin B. **A History of the Movies.** 1931.

Hardy, Forsyth. **Scandinavian Film.** 1952.

Hepworth, Cecil M. **Animated Photography: The A B C of the Cinematograph.** 1900.

Hoban, Charles F., Jr., and Edward B. Van Ormer. **Instructional Film Research 1918-1950.** 1950.

Holaday, Perry W. and George D. Stoddard. **Getting Ideas from the Movies.** 1933.

Hopwood, Henry V. **Living Pictures.** 1899.

Hulfish, David S. **Motion-Picture Work.** 1915.

Hunter, William. **Scrutiny of Cinema.** 1932.

Huntley, John. **British Film Music.** 1948.

Irwin, Will. **The House That Shadows Built.** 1928.

Jarratt, Vernon. **The Italian Cinema.** 1951.

Jenkins, C. Francis. **Animated Pictures.** 1898.

Lang, Edith and George West. **Musical Accompaniment of Moving Pictures.** 1920.

London, Kurt. **Film Music.** 1936.

Lutz, E [dwin] G [eorge]. **The Motion-Picture Cameraman.** 1927.

Manvell, Roger. **Experiment in the Film.** 1949.

Marey, Etienne Jules. **Movement.** 1895.

Martin, Olga J. **Hollywood's Movie Commandments.** 1937.

Mayer, J. P. **Sociology of Film: Studies and Documents.** 1946. New Introduction by J. P. Mayer.

Münsterberg, Hugo. **The Photoplay: A Psychological Study.** 1916.
Nicoll, Allardyce. **Film and Theatre.** 1936.

Noble, Peter. **The Negro in Films.** 1949.

Peters, Charles C. **Motion Pictures and Standards of Morality.** 1933.

Peterson, Ruth C. and L. L. Thurstone. **Motion Pictures and the Social Attitudes of Children.** Shuttleworth, Frank K. and Mark A. May. **The Social Conduct and Attitudes of Movie Fans.** 1933.

Phillips, Henry Albert. **The Photodrama.** 1914.

Photoplay Research Society. **Opportunities in the Motion Picture Industry.** 1922.

Rapée, Erno. **Encyclopaedia of Music for Pictures.** 1925.

Rapée, Erno. **Motion Picture Moods for Pianists and Organists.** 1924.

Renshaw, Samuel, Vernon L. Miller and Dorothy P. Marquis. **Children's Sleep.** 1933.

Rosten, Leo C. Hollywood: The Movie Colony, The Movie Makers. 1941.

Sadoul, Georges. French Film. 1953.

Screen Monographs I, 1923-1937. 1970.

Screen Monographs II, 1915-1930. 1970.

Sinclair, Upton. Upton Sinclair Presents William Fox. 1933.

Talbot, Frederick A. Moving Pictures. 1912.

Thorp, Margaret Farrand. America at the Movies. 1939.

Wollenberg, H. H. Fifty Years of German Film. 1948.

RELATED BOOKS AND PERIODICALS

Allister, Ray. Friese-Greene: Close-Up of an Inventor. 1948.

Art in Cinema: A Symposium of the Avant-Garde Film, edited by Frank Stauffacher. 1947.

The Art of Cinema: Selected Essays. New Foreword by George Amberg. 1971.

Balázs, Béla. Theory of the Film. 1952.

Barry, Iris. Let's Go to the Movies. 1926.

de Beauvoir, Simone. Brigitte Bardot and the Lolita Syndrome. 1960.

Carrick, Edward. Art and Design in the British Film. 1948.

Close Up. Vols. 1-10, 1927-1933 (all published).

Cogley, John. Report on Blacklisting. Part I: The Movies. 1956.

Eisenstein, S. M. Que Viva Mexico! 1951.

Experimental Cinema. 1930-1934 (all published).

Feldman, Joseph and Harry. Dynamics of the Film. 1952.

Film Daily Yearbook of Motion Pictures. Microfilm, 18 reels, 35 mm. 1918-1969.

Film Daily Yearbook of Motion Pictures. 1970.

Film Daily Yearbook of Motion Pictures. (Wid's Year Book). 3 vols., 1918-1922.

The Film Index: A Bibliography. Vol. I: The Film as Art. 1941.

Film Society Programmes. 1925-1939 (all published).

Films: A Quarterly of Discussion and Analysis. Nos. 1-4, 1939-1940 (all published).

Flaherty, Frances Hubbard. The Odyssey of a Film-Maker: Robert Flaherty's Story. 1960.

General Bibliography of Motion Pictures, edited by Carl Vincent, Riccardo Redi, and Franco Venturini. 1953.

Hendricks, Gordon. Origins of the American Film. 1961-1966. New Introduction by Gordon Hendricks.

Hound and Horn: Essays on Cinema, 1928-1934. 1971.

Huff, Theodore. **Charlie Chaplin.** 1951.

Kahn, Gordon. **Hollywood on Trial.** 1948.

New York Times Film Reviews, 1913-1968. 1970.

Noble, Peter. **Hollywood Scapegoat: The Biography of Erich von Stroheim.** 1950.

Robson, E. W. and M. M. **The Film Answers Back.** 1939.

Seldes, Gilbert. **An Hour with the Movies and the Talkies.** 1929.

Weinberg, Herman G., editor. **Greed.** 1971.

Wollenberg, H. H. **Anatomy of the Film.** 1947.

Wright, Basil. **The Use of the Film.** 1948.

DISSERTATIONS ON FILM

Karpf, Stephen L. **The Gangster Film: Emergence, Variation and Decay of a Genre, 1930-1940.** First publication, 1973.

Lounsbury, Myron O. **The Origins of American Film Criticism, 1909-1939.** First publication, 1973.

Sands, Pierre N. **A Historical Study of the Academy of the Motion Picture Arts and Sciences (1927-1947).** First publication, 1973.

North, Joseph H. **The Early Development of the Motion Picture, 1887-1909.** First publication, 1973.

Rimberg, John. **The Motion Picture in the Soviet Union, 1918-1952.** First publication, 1973.

Wolfe, Glenn J. **Vachel Lindsay: The Poet as Film Theorist.** First publication, 1973.